D1602782

An Osage Journey to Europe, 1827–1830

THE AMERICAN EXPLORATION AND TRAVEL SERIES

Unattributed illustration, "Osages, Indians arrived in Paris 13 August 1827." Probably produced, independently of a booklet, for sale as an individual print. Missouri History Museum, St. Louis.

An Osage Journey to Europe, 1827–1830

Three French Accounts

EDITED AND TRANSLATED BY

William Least Heat-Moon

AND

James K. Wallace

UNIVERSITY OF OKLAHOMA PRESS : NORMAN

Also by William Least Heat-Moon
Blue Highways: A Journey into America (Boston, 1982)
PrairyErth (a deep map) (Boston, 1991)
River-Horse: The Logbook of a Boat across America (Boston, 1999)
Roads to Quoz: An American Mosey (New York, 2008)
Christopher Columbus in the Americas (Hoboken, N.J., 2002)
Here, There, Elsewhere: Stories from the Road (New York, 2013)

Publication of this book is made possible through the generosity of Edith Kinney Gaylord.

Library of Congress Cataloging-in-Publication Data
Heat Moon, William Least.
An Osage journey to Europe, 1827–1830: three French accounts / edited and translated by William Least Heat-Moon and James K. Wallace.
    pages   cm.
(The American exploration and travel series; volume 81)
Includes bibliographical references and index.
ISBN 978-0-8061-4403-0 (hardcover: alk. paper)
1. Osage Indians—Travel—France—History—19th century. 2.Osage Indians—Relocation—France—History—19th century. 3.Osage Indians—France—Public opinion. 4. Indians in popular culture—History—19th century. 5. Public opinion—France—History—19th century. I. Title.
E99.O8H43 2013
978.004'975254 2—dc23
                        2013009689

An Osage Journey to Europe, 1827–1830: Three French Accounts
is Volume 81 in The American Exploration and Travel Series.

The paper in this book meets the guidelines for permanence and durability of the Committee on Production Guidelines for Book Longevity of the Council on Library Resources, Inc. ∞

1 2 3 4 5 6 7 8 9 10

Contents

Illustrations

Figures

Color Plates

Preface

A Thousand-Dollar Book

SOME TWENTY YEARS AGO I came across a bookseller offering a volume I had never known about, *Histoire de la Tribu des Osages*, by a mysterious "M. P. V." and printed in Paris in 1827. Although bound in fragile paper covers, the text was on hearty stock. At nearly a thousand dollars for the ninety-two pages—almost ten dollars a page—the book was beyond my means.

In the days before computer-driven searching, I rather laboriously looked into the *Histoire* and discovered it was indeed rare and had never been published in English. I persuaded the good-natured bookseller to let me borrow his copy so that I might evaluate it and decide whether to have a go at translating what appeared to be a good story, and to make it readily available for scholars, lay readers, and the Osage people themselves.

As I began working with the text, I learned that M. P. V. was Monsieur Paul Vissier but discovered nothing more about him other than that he was educated—perhaps a professor or *philosophe*—and lived in or near Paris. I also realized my French was too far behind to allow me to make a reliable translation, so I asked a friend in the Romance Languages Department of the University of Missouri if he would take a look at Vissier's text. As James Wallace read, he became progressively more interested and wondered: What was the unnamed work Vissier continually refers to, and who was its author he nitpicks—despite his own misunderstandings—and sarcastically castigates?

Over the several years it took all this to unfold, I stumbled across the title of the mystery work Vissier criticized, and not long thereafter Wallace turned up a library copy of it—a thirty-eight-page pamphlet titled *Six Indiens Rouges*, author unknown. All along, one of the booklets had been just across town in the State Historical Society of Missouri, but until finding elsewhere the link between the two works, I could not know that. Professor Emeritus Wallace by then had retired to open a bookshop—Possum Haw Antiquarians—in the courthouse-square town of Fayette, Missouri, and he searched the market unsuccessfully for copies of both the *Histoire* and *Six Indiens*. The rarity and historical import of the publications confirmed my thought of the two of us bringing these works into an annotated version in English.

In both books the information about the Children of the Middle Waters—as the Osage sometimes style themselves—is revealing. But perhaps as significant is the story behind their European travels and the touching picture it reveals about European perceptions of—to use the French term of that time—*sauvages*, as well as the events of their tour that triggered both works. The 1827 transatlantic journey of a half-dozen "Missouri Majesties," a term some nineteenth-century French writers used, is a tale of triumph descending into destitution, with both aspects manifesting European responses not only toward the Osages but toward so-called *primitifs* around the globe.

Six Red Indians and *The History of the Osage Tribe*—and to a much lesser degree, their progenitor, John Dunn Hunter's *Memoirs of a Captivity*—are the earliest works presenting in a systematic manner a cultural history of the Osage tribe. Incipient if rudimentary, the booklets present some details and interpretations that do not square with contemporary tribal notions or current anthropological studies. Nevertheless, errors, misapprehensions, and misrepresentations sometimes explain history more fully than circumscribing accuracy. In addition to presenting reliable versions of these pamphlets deserving a wider readership, we want to amplify—as much as possible after almost two centuries—the Osage tour that precipitated the works. To that end we have included another text we only recently discovered: *Remarks About the Six Indians*, also published anonymously in Paris right after the arrival of the Osages in France.

Our goal is to set forth these works in annotated translations for both the general reader as well as the specialist who may wish to evaluate the accuracy of each detail about nineteenth-century Osage life offered by the three French authors.

Despite several years of looking, we still have questions concerning these publications—many of which will not likely ever find answers. Yet we believe the three related booklets of cultural history are valuable additions to the history of the Osage people and stand at the center of an affecting story about the ways two cultures, so strange to each other, reacted when they came face to face.

William Least Heat-Moon
February 2011

Acknowledgments

For their informed assistance we thank Todd Christine, Laura Jolley, Kimberly Harper, Sara Przybylski, Gwendolyn Gray, June DeWeese, Tyler Dwyer, Nina Sappington, Amit Bosu, R. Bruce McMillan, W. Raymond Wood, Kelly Archer, Stephen Archer, Sarah Cash, Bonnie Coles, Sandy Schiefer, Lyn Fredericksen, Mélanie Westbrook, Olaf Schmidt, L. Hunter Kevil, Delores Fisher, Helen Long, Jill Gage, Kay Wisnia, Judy Brown, Mary Ellen Brooks, Chris Dunn, Stuart Hinds, Teresa Gipson, Scott Gipson, Bruce Sherwood, Kelly McEniry, John Finley, Dennis Northcott, J. B. Waggoner, James R. Akerman, Kathryn Wallace, and Jo Ann Trogdon.

We appreciate the help of The State Historical Society of Missouri; Ellis Library of the University of Missouri; Nichols Library of the University of Missouri-Kansas City; The Newberry Library, Chicago; Denver Public Library; Science Library of the University of Georgia; Smiley Library of Central Methodist University; Osage Tribal Museum, Pawhuska, Oklahoma; The Corcoran Gallery of Art, Washington, D.C.; and the Gilcrease Institute, Tulsa, Oklahoma.

At the University of Oklahoma Press, we thank Chuck Rankin, Robert Clark, and Emily Jerman. We also thank copyeditor Stacy Moran and indexer Sherrye Young.

An Osage Journey to Europe, 1827–1830

Introduction

The Inception

IN 1493, ON THE RETURN from his initial voyage to what he thought was the East Indies, Christopher Columbus brought the first indigenous people of the New World to Europe for display. With him aboard the *Niña* were six Taino men apparently curious about an exotic world beyond their Caribbean islands. Seeing the "Indians" in their full native regalia, Queen Isabella was moved enough by their humanity that she would later discourage the importation of indigenous Americans for the European slave market—but not before Columbus, on his second voyage, captured and carried back for the block several hundred Native people, virtually all of whom soon died.

Almost a century and a quarter later, in 1616, John Rolfe, an English colonizer at Jamestown, Virginia, returned to London with his Algonquin wife, Matoaka, better known by her nickname, Pocahontas. She became a sensation at the court of James I but also did not long survive Old World diseases.

Over the following century, the European fascination with aboriginal Americans continued with other tribal members under various auspices making trips to the Continent. The first Osage visitor to France was a chief who had been living with his people in central Missouri. He accompanied a Missouria woman and three other chieftains of the Oto, Illinois, and Missouria tribes. The group was assembled by Étienne de Veniard, Sieur de Bourgmont, the first white man to explore the lower Missouri Valley in an organized way and to report on his findings. As the founder of Fort Orleans in 1723–24 on the lower Missouri River, he established relations with the Indians—the Osages in particular—which led to commercial exchanges that endured into the early years of American sovereignty. On the Osage chief's return to the tribe, his evocative recountings about his travels across "the great lake" planted the idea in his young warriors for a second crossing. It took 102 years before the idea reached fulfillment. This later 1827 entourage, composed of four men and two women (who ventured to France, Belgium, the Netherlands, Germany, Switzerland, and Italy), is the subject of *An Osage Journey to Europe, 1827–1830*.

The spokesman and most honored warrior of the travelers was Little Chief, who said he was a descendant of the man who visited the court of the king of France a century earlier.[1] While Little Chief's interest in following in ancestral footsteps was possibly the initial reason for the trip, it was, according to Paul Vissier in his *History of the Tribe of the Osages*, David Delaunay, a Frenchman then living in St. Louis, who assisted—and probably encouraged—the Indians to travel abroad by solving the logistics for their passage.

Twenty-five Osages, writes Vissier, had spent the previous four years hunting furs to have money enough for the journey. Early in 1827 twelve of them set off down the wild Missouri River only to lose all their furs, baggage, and money in a "raft" mishap somewhere west of St. Louis; the accident apparently caused six of them to decide against making the oceanic crossing. Upon arriving in what the French sometimes referred to as Fort St. Louis, the Osages called upon Delaunay (so he apparently told Vissier) to include them on his own forthcoming trip to France. As director of the tour, Delaunay added François Tesson as codirector of management. The third member was interpreter Paul Loise. Delaunay either raised funds for six of the Osages to travel down the Mississippi on the steamboat *Commerce*, or he persuaded the captain to grant them free passage to New Orleans. Built in 1826 in Pittsburgh, the *Commerce* was a side-wheel merchant vessel plying a route between St. Louis and the Crescent City. It is likely the six Osages traveled as deck passengers, finding space where they could among the stacks of freight, and they

---

1. In several places in all French texts, the identification of this king is mistakenly given as either Louis XIV or Louis XVI; correctly, in 1725, the king of France was Louis XV. See note 41 to *Six Red Indians*.

may have helped defray the cost of their passage by assisting the crew in moving cargo and bringing on board cords of wood needed for the boilers. Delaunay, it would seem, booked a cabin with furnished meals for the seven-day passage to New Orleans.

While in the city, the Osages happened upon, perhaps through Delaunay, Matthew B. Anduze, a French missionary whom they apparently had met in the western country. Because Anduze was immediately bound for France, Little Chief asked the missionary to prepare the way for them. On May 29, 1827, they departed for France on the American ship *New-England*. The passage, described by Vissier as "a long and difficult voyage," took almost two months.

Father Anduze evidently had followed through with advance preparations for the Osages because upon arrival of the *New-England* in Le Havre on July 27, the docks were crowded with gawkers, some of whom climbed onto spars and into the rigging of nearby ships to catch a glimpse of the strange and colorfully attired *sauvages*. Eleven days later, to avoid a milling throng waiting at the dock, the riverboat carrying the Osages to Rouen halted three miles above the city and put them in a carriage to get them to their hotel, where a contingent of the royal guard was posted at their door. Details of this early leg of the trip appear in the conclusions to *Six Red Indians*, Vissier's *History*, and throughout *Remarks about the Six Indians*.

The Travelers

While reliable information about the nine people who undertook the long journey is limited, enough details—including several portraits—have survived the erasures of time to distinguish each of the travelers from the others. Indeed, one of the remarkable aspects of the Osages' European tour is the number of portraits made of the Indians, so that today we have a good idea of what they looked like. Accompanying Delaunay, Loise, and Tesson were Little Chief, Black Bird (or Black Spirit), Young Soldier (or The Little Soldier), Big Soldier, Sacred Sun (or Mohongo), and Hawk Woman.

Little Chief,[2] variously represented in Osage as Kishagashugah or

---

2. See Paul Wilhelm's comment on the names of the travelers in appendix C.

Kihegashugah or Ke-He-Kah Shinkah or Cashunghia, was reportedly the great-grandson of the Osage man who visited France in 1725.
Born about 1791, Little Chief was thirty-five or thirty-six years old at
the start of the journey. The second chief of his village, he was the
tallest and most distinguished of the men; one Parisian commented
that "he had a little more nobility in his gestures and walk than the
others." Although not the senior member of the Osage contingent or
the one the French called "The Orator," Little Chief was the spokesman for the entourage. The author of *Remarks*, who says he spent
time with the Osages, mentions Little Chief as being the spouse of
Hawk Woman, who appears with him (and Young Soldier) in the
superb Louis-Léopold Boilly montage portraits (see color gallery, p.
29). Given that Indian marital rites were less restrictive than those
of Europeans and Americans, that the two women were only about
eighteen at the beginning of the voyage, and that Sacred Sun gave
birth in Europe, any "marital" ties may have been coincident with the
trip itself or merely assumed for the convenience of European pro-
priety. (See the section titled "Marriages" in *Six Indians*.)

In Paris, a highlight, if we may use that word, was a ride in a hot
air balloon by Little Chief, who, being a member of the Eagle clan,
startled everyone as he ascended with "a piercing and savage chant,"
which Osage historian John Joseph Mathews interprets as "a prayer-
song . . . asking for the power to stay afloat."[3]

One modern account, confusing him with Little Soldier, mentions
Little Chief dying of smallpox on the return voyage, but in fact he
participated in treaty councils at Fort Gibson in Indian Territory in
1833 and 1839, the latter council almost a decade after the return of
the group to America.

Black Bird or Black Spirit—in Osage, Washing-Sahba or Wash-
inka-Sabe or Waschingsabhe—was born about 1795. A respected
warrior, he was second in command to Little Chief. About thirty-
two years old upon arrival in France, he may have been Sacred Sun's
mate. Reportedly he was one of the two Osages who died of smallpox aboard ship and was buried at sea on the return voyage in 1830.

---

3. Mathews, *The Osages*, 544.

Of the six Indians, Black Spirit is the only one for whom we have not found a skilled pictorial rendering.

Although Joseph Mathews says the Osage name of Young Soldier—Mink-chatahook or Minckcha-tagonh or Minck-Chatahooh—is not translatable,[4] in the French texts here, he is sometimes called *Le Petit Soldat*, The Little Soldier. Born about 1805, he was twenty-two years old at the start of the journey. According to Mathews, who drew upon Osage oral history in the 1960s, Young Soldier was the other person to die of smallpox on the return voyage.

Big Soldier—Marchar-Kitah-Toonhah or Mo'n-Sho'n A-ki-da Tonkah and several other variations—was the eldest member of the group at about forty-eight years old. In some ways he was the most interesting because of varying interpretations of his character, the import of his name, and especially his longevity, which led to later encounters with travelers to Indian Territory. The French sometimes referred to him as *L'Orateur*, The Orator, perhaps because of his alleged volubility, a detail coinciding with one interpretation of his role among his people both in America and France. In later years, Edward Chouteau of the famous St. Louis trading family told Victor Tixier, who recorded their conversation in his *Travels on the Osage Prairies*, that Big Soldier was nothing more than a *marmiton*—French for a scullery menial.[5] Yet another French traveler, Louis Richard Cortambert, who met Little Chief and Sacred Sun in the Osage country in 1833, wrote in his "Journey to the Land of the Osages" that a marmiton was "an important personnage in every village . . . [who] knows all that happens [and] is the village newspaper."[6] Of the early writers commenting on Big Soldier, Cortambert also uses the term marmiton, perhaps inaccurately. Washington Irving, in one of his journal notes he relied on to write his popular *Tour on the Prairies*, says: "Chief cook of Osage villages—a great dignitary—combining grand chamberlain, minister of state, master of ceremonies and town crier—has under-cooks. He tastes broth &. When strangers arrive he goes about the village and makes proclamation—great white man,

---

4. Ibid, 541.
5. Tixier, *Tixier's Travels*, 98–99.
6. Cortambert, "Journey to the Land of the Osages," 216–17.

great chief arrived—warriors turn out and prepare to receive him properly. Chief lodge prepared for reception—mats placed, etc."[7]

And, not to be ignored is Vissier's extended comment on "Cooks" in his chapter 10. If it is true that Big Soldier, as he preferred to represent himself, put on airs and often tried to enhance his own status, such behavior would not be entirely inappropriate, given his accomplishments as a leader in battles and in treaty councils.

Contemporaneous French reports commented on his stately bearing and described him as "dignified"—perceptions that do not necessarily negate Mathews's view that Big Soldier was "possibly a Nobody strutting before Gallic enthusiasm."[8] Yet, he received a medal for bravery from the Spanish before the Louisiana Purchase, and Vissier says Big Soldier distinguished himself in battle. In 1804 and 1806 he traveled to Washington City where he met President Jefferson, who was then intent on moving the Osages off their ancestral lands. Explorer Zebulon Pike appointed him leader of the Osage contingent in his 1806 expedition, and George Sibley, the factor at Fort Osage on the Missouri River, considered Big Soldier to be among the most influential warriors in the tribe and a man of good sense, but not always "firm" in his actions.

Although he supported cooperation with Americans, when it became clear that U.S. policies were creating social and economic ruination among the Osages, The Orator movingly told Sibley in 1820:

> I see and admire your manner of living, your good warm houses, your extensive fields of corn, your gardens, your cows, oxen, work horses, wagons, and a thousand machines I know not the use of. I see that you are able to clothe yourself, even from weeds and grass. In short, you can do almost what you choose. You whites possess the power of subduing almost every animal to your use. You are surrounded by slaves. Everything about you is in chains, and you are slaves yourselves. I hear I should exchange my presents for yours. [Then] I too should become a slave. Talk to my sons, perhaps they may be persuaded to adopt

---

7. *The Western Journals of Washington Irving*, 135.
8. Mathews, *The Osages*, 540.

your fashions, or at least to recommend them to their sons; but for myself, I was born free, was raised free, and wish to die free. I am perfectly content with my condition.[9]

To look at his distinguished profile painted by Charles de Saint-Mémin in 1804 or the later portrait by John Mix Stanley of 1843, one can readily imagine his capacity to impress an audience. Stanley, who spent a week with him, said Big Soldier at the age of seventy performed "in the various dances and amusements with as much zest as any of the young warriors."[10] He died the next year.

Sacred Sun or Mohongo—also Myhangah or Mi-Ho'n-Ga—was about eighteen years old and may have been the spouse of Black Bird and a relative of Hawk Woman. In their book, *Into the Spotlight: Four Missouri Women*, Margot Ford McMillen and Heather Roberson offer evidence that Sacred Sun was later a "country wife" of one of the Chouteaus, and by him had a daughter; the names of both mother and daughter appear in an 1825 treaty. While in Belgium on February 10, 1828, Mohongo gave birth to twin girls, Maria-Theresa and Maria-Elizabeth, the former adopted by a Belgian woman of means. This child died the next year, but Maria-Elizabeth survived to reach the United States and be painted sitting on her mother's lap by Charles Bird King in Washington City in 1830. Thomas L. McKenney, the head of Indian Affairs, wrote a brief sketch about Sacred Sun—paired with King's well-known portrait of her and her daughter—that appeared in his celebrated book *The Indian Tribes of North America*. They both returned to the Osage villages along the Neosho River near Fort Gibson in what is today Oklahoma. In 1836 McKenney informed William Clark that Mohongo had died of smallpox.

Hawk Woman—Gretomih or Grothomil or Gthe-Do'n-Wi'n—was born about 1809 and by several accounts was related to Sacred Sun. The author of *Remarks* says she was the eighteen-year-old cousin and wife of Little Chief, but other reports have her as the spouse of Little Soldier. McKenney's essay "Mohongo" says Hawk Woman was a cousin—not spouse—of Little Chief, and indeed they

9. Quoted in Peake, *History of the United States Indian Factory System*, 229–30.
10. Stanley, *Smithsonian Miscellaneous Collections*, 44.

did return together on the same ship in 1830 after the Osages divided into two groups. While in Switzerland, perhaps to raise money or for a gift, she made two belts of braided European red wool, elaborately decorated with strung white glass beads. A 1908 article in *American Anthropologist* mentions two of her belts being in the Bern Museum.

Of the non-Osage participants on the European tour, director David Delaunay's role and character are most problematic. The dominant question is: as director, did he exploit the Osages and later abandon them in Europe? Exploitation and abandonment are pejorative words with definitions depending on a point of view. If we change the questions to did Delaunay wish to make money from the tour, and did he leave the group after some months, then the answer to both is *yes*. But a departure is not necessarily an abandonment, and making money as a showman is not in itself exploitation, especially when, as in this case, the Osages themselves were willing participants also hoping for compensation. Even McKenney, a nemesis of Delaunay, could write in his sketch of Mohongo: "It is obvious that [the Osages'] own views were mercenary, and that they were incited to travel by the alleged value of the presents which would probably be made them."[11]

Delaunay was born in France but by the start of the Osage tour had been in St. Louis a quarter of a century. He had some connections with Spain during its years of hegemony in the Louisiana Territory, and subsequently he became the adjutant general of the territorial militia; Vissier and others refer to him as Colonel Delaunay, and the author of *Remarks* refers to him prior to 1792 as an officer under Louis XVI. In 1804, six days after the Corps of Discovery began heading up the Missouri on its great western expedition, William Clark noted in his journal a visit to the St. Charles encampment by "Several Gentlemen."[12] Among them were respected merchants, a French scientist, and two judges, one of whom was Delaunay, then an associate justice in the new Court of Quarter Sessions in nearby St. Louis. He was also an associate of the influential Auguste Chouteau.

In 1800, during the Spanish regime in the Missouri country,

---

11. McKenney, *History of the Indian Tribes*, 44.
12. *The Journals of the Lewis & Clark Expedition*, Moulton ed., Volume 2, 243.

Delaunay received a large land grant, and after the Americans bought the territory, he was appointed in 1812 to a governmental committee along with several others including Alexander McNair, who in 1821 would become the first governor once Missouri was admitted into the Union. Also in 1812, Delaunay oversaw the settlement of Meriwether Lewis's estate, a most significant task.

On at least two occasions, Delaunay had problems with indebtedness. In Missouri, after his departure for Europe, he and his wife Eleanore were beset by an 1828 mortgage foreclosure. The second issue cropped up in France over an old debt of some 9,000 francs incurred in 1799, apparently not long before he came to America. This latter incident involved a former business associate's widow, who had Delaunay jailed in Paris until he made some sort of restitution to gain his freedom and continue the Osage tour. Was Delaunay indeed a man of questionable business ethics, as some contemporaneous European news accounts claimed, or rather, was he a poor manager of money, as the Missouri mortgage foreclosure suggests?

In Ghent, Belgium, in early 1828, Delaunay brought a libel suit against a respected editor of the newspaper *La Sentinelle*. The trial drew a large crowd fixed upon gaping at the Osage travelers who arrived to give testimony, attired as always in their striking Native dress. Their interpreter was Father Charles de la Croix, a former missionary the Indians knew and greeted with pleasure. Black Bird offered to the court that Delaunay kept the group well fed and did not hold them in bondage, as a chambermaid had suggested. Even McKenney would later write of the Osage travelers: "They profess to have been on the whole gratified with the expedition."[13]

In his testimony, Paul Loise said the Osages initially undertook the tour out of curiosity and only later for financial gain. He stated that Delaunay received all proceeds, which would be divided among the Osages upon their return home, adding that they had bought numerous items in Paris, an indication of some distribution of money to the Osages while in Europe.

The public prosecutor's argument that the accusing editor had slandered "the brave Colonel Delaunay" and exposed him to contempt car-

---

13. McKenney, *History of the Indian Tribes*, 46.

ried the judgment. The editor, "a distinguished literary man," was found guilty and received a sentence of six weeks in prison, a fine of three hundred florins, and the loss of his civil rights for five years. Foreigner Delaunay's decisive victory over an esteemed local man is significant. Of the many charges brought against him in European newspapers, the Ghent trial was the only instance of accusations being critically examined and Delaunay being allowed to defend himself. Its outcome seems to dismiss—or at least tone down—assertions of his malfeasance.

Unquestionably, Delaunay was adept at bringing often overwhelming attention to the Osages and even managed to gain them an audience with King Charles X. But it appears that his arrest for the 1799 debt and, even more, a gradually waning interest in the tour eventually led to his departure. After early 1829, we have found only one subsequent mention of his association with the group—when he may have left the Osages while in Breslau, Prussia—and his disappearance, whenever it occurred, is one of the mysteries of the thirty-seven-month tour. Apparently, he did not return to the United States.

McKenney's essay on Sacred Sun impugned Delaunay's motives and character, interpretations picked up by later commentators. McKenney claimed that Delaunay, without authorization, led the Osages to believe their visit had official sanction; to McKenney, Delaunay, beyond being a poseur, inveigled them into the trip for his own financial gain. McKenney's commentary on Sacred Sun, however, is something of a distortion because of its promulgating his deep belief that Euro-American civilization was a benefit to Indians and would help them emerge from a perceived barbarism. The piece is condescending, marginally racist, and its cultural generalizations—often set forth in depreciatory terms—have the inaccuracy common to broad generalities.

We have found only a single reference to an Osage complaint about the European tour: in his *Travels on the Osage Prairies*, Victor Tixier mentions Big Soldier in 1840, ten years after the trip, grumbling over the loss of his possessions in Europe and vaguely about "the person who had taken him to France."[14]

The role of interpreter Paul Loise during the Osage journey has

---

14. Tixier, *Tixier's Travels*, 99.

Charles Willson Peale's 1806 silhouette of Paul Loise
(Paul Chouteau), probably cut in Philadelphia. Author's collection.

received scant attention despite his being with the travelers for the three years following the St. Louis departure until the return there. Of the many assertions about him from both his contemporaries and modern commentators, there is little consensus, an unfortunate fact in that Loise not only was the lone person to accompany the Osage entourage virtually the entire time (despite occasional days on his own), but he also provided information for the news accounts and several pamphlets, including the three featured here.

Born in 1775, he was fifty-two years old in 1827. According to *Six Red Indians*, he was the son of a Frenchman living in America and an Osage woman, but other sources say his parents were a Frenchman living in St. Louis and a French-born woman. Yet other accounts suggest his father was a Chouteau—either Auguste or Pierre—and his mother an Osage "country wife" living in the western outback, and, in fact, he was also known as Paul Chouteau (not to be confused with Paul Liguest Chouteau, born in 1792). Loise may have been adopted by Pierre Chouteau, who later put him on his payroll. His witnessing of treaties with an X indicates he was illiterate although trilingual: English, French, and Osage.

Loise accompanied the important Osage delegation of 1806 (and possibly others) to Washington and on to Philadelphia, where Charles Willson Peale made a silhouette of him, the only known image of one of the three non-Osage men on the European tour.

In 1808, the governor of Missouri Territory, Meriwether Lewis, appointed him as interpreter for the Osage tribe, a role he fulfilled at treaty councils that year and again in 1818, with both of those treaties ceding Osage land. An 1808 letter Lewis wrote to President Thomas Jefferson expressed his belief that Loise would translate faithfully.[15] Another missive, this one from Secretary of War Henry Dearborn, says, "We have made young Paul Chouteau a chief of the Little Osages."[16] The employment of Loise during several important treaties between 1815 and 1825 suggests William Clark had trust in the interpreter's ability and perhaps also belief in Loise's integrity—or at least his alliance with federal interests.

In early 1827, an agent to the Osage tribe, I. F. Hamtramck, wrote that he ordered Loise off the reserve for fear of his influence on the proposed trip; he claimed Loise hid in the woods until Hamtramck's departure, when Loise returned and assisted or "induced" several Osages to strike out with their furs toward St. Louis.[17] If Paul Vissier is correct in his assertion that to underwrite their travel, two dozen Osages hunted pelts for four years prior to their voyage to Europe, then Loise's influence as an instigator seems dubious. More probable is that he assisted some of the Osages who had reasons of their own for a European visit; one personal motivation is evident in Little Chief's assertion five years after his return from France, a time when the disintegration of the old Native ways was most evident: "I have

15. Lewis, *American State Papers: Indian Affairs*, Volume 1, 766.
16. Quoted in *Letters of the Lewis and Clark Expedition*, Volume 1, 305.
17. Grant Foreman, "Our Indian Ambassadors," 113–14.

traveled all over the world to learn the means to render my people happy, without success."[18] None of this, of course, denies that all participants—French and Osage—in their long-established entrepreneurial relationships hoped to gain materially from the visit.

Once Loise reached Europe, some local observers saw him as an exploiter, while others considered him a guide whom the Osages trusted. In 1829 the American consul in Paris, Isaac Cox Barnet, wrote Secretary of State Martin Van Buren of his belief in Loise's "cupidity,"[19] yet at about the same time Vicomte de Gironde sent a letter affirming that Loise appeared devoted to the Osages. Bishop William Du Bourg also offered his confidence in Loise's honesty and his trustworthiness in assisting the Osages' return to America. A notice in *Niles' Weekly Register* for September 5, 1829, says Loise "remained faithful to [the Osages], and returned with them."

In his essay about the tour, Grant Foreman presents some ambiguous evidence that Loise may have been the father of Sacred Sun's twin daughters; possible substantiation might be in the description of one of the infants having a lighter complexion than her sister. Indeed, when Loise and his thirteen-year-old son (who only late and briefly appears in the overseas story) returned to America, they were on the same ship as Sacred Sun and her daughter rather than with the others who sailed later from Bordeaux. In a June 1830 letter to Thomas McKenney, William Clark wrote from St. Louis: "I have sent the Osages who returned from France, to their Nation, except Paul Loese, who was not willing to go further than this place, fearing the vengeance of the Relations of the two Osages who died on the passage home."[20] But that assertion hardly confirms malfeasance. That some Osages would be unwilling or unable to understand that the interpreter had nothing to do with smallpox seems obvious, as does the fact that Loise's family was apparently elsewhere. He died in 1832, at about fifty-seven.

Finally, the role of the third non-Osage participant, François

---

18. Quoted in McMillen and Robertson, *Into the Spotlight*, 33.

19. Quoted in Carolyn Foreman, *Indians Abroad*, 144.

20. Superintendent of Indian Affairs, St. Louis Records, 1897–1855, Volume 4, 15 May 1830, 119–20.

Tesson, appears to have been minimal, with mention of him rarely coming up in reports at the time of the journey. In 1827, there were, minimally, four men in St. Louis named François Tesson. Their births were progressively about a decade apart, with the youngest in his twenties and the oldest fifty-seven, the latter dying the year the Osages left for Europe. Had he died overseas, one would expect that to have been reported. Because Tesson was an American, it would seem he returned to the United States, but we have found no such record.

The Travels in Europe

In America, the French, including those from Canada, generally found more amicable and productive ways of working and living with the Osages than did either the British or Americans. The lucrative fur trade that built St. Louis and turned the Osages into the most powerful tribe in the lower Missouri Valley—both economically and in force of arms—was the result of successful collaborations between French of all stripes and the Osages. Following the Louisiana Purchase in 1803, as Americans came to power along the Missouri, the fortunes of the tribe began a descent. In 1808 William Clark helped negotiate a treaty extinguishing the Osage right of occupancy in an immense portion of Missouri and a good piece of Arkansas—almost fifty-five million acres—to open their lands to both Americans and eastern tribes. Additional treaties in 1818 and 1825 completed the forced move of the Osages westward, so reducing their power and influence that William Clark would write in 1826: "Their power has been broken, their warlike spirit subdued, and themselves sunk into objects of pity and commiseration. While strong and hostile, it has been our obvious policy to weaken them; now that they are weak and harmless, and most of their lands fallen into our hands, justice and humanity require us to cherish and befriend them."[21]

Some years later, Major-General Ethan Allen Hitchcock wrote in his *A Traveler in Indian Territory* that Clark believed "if he was to be

---

21. Quoted in Buckley, *William Clark, Indian Diplomat*, 166.

damned hereafter it would be for making that treaty."[22]

While their influence lasted, the French, despite the failure of their hope of gaining lasting dominion in the lower Missouri Valley, achieved successful entrepreneurial, cultural, and marital relationships through traders and missionaries so that many Osage saw the French among them as economic partners, friends, and even relatives. The scholarly Jesuits were particularly active in establishing a reasonable rapport and creating an Osage interest in France itself, thereby helping foster the atmosphere leading to the 1827 visit to seven European countries.

In France, curiosity about indigenous Americans gained impetus from the notion of the so-called Noble Savage, popularized by Jean-Jacques Rousseau in 1750 in his seminal essay addressing a question publicly put forth: do the arts and sciences contribute to an improved morality? Rousseau's eloquent *Non!* was taken up by poets, painters, and philosophers, all of whom began reconsidering soi-disant "primitive" peoples around the globe, none more deeply linked to France than the Osages. Rousseau's notions[23] on that topic were hardly those evinced by McKenney.

A year earlier, the first volume of another work of more or less equal influence appeared. The natural historian George-Louis Leclerc, better known today as Count Buffon, began publishing his multivolume, encyclopedic *Histoire naturelle*. In it he presented a theory of degeneracy in New World species from insects to human beings. He believed all were weaker and smaller than the creatures of the Old World, a result of living in—as he presumed—a wet and cold climate, a realm the count had never seen. In *Mr. Jefferson and the Giant Moose*, biologist Lee Alan Dugatkin writes: "For Buffon, Indians were stupid, lazy savages. In a particularly emasculating swipe, he suggested that the genitalia of Indian males were small and withered—degenerate—for the very same reason that the people

---

22. Hitchcock, *Traveler in Indian Territory*, 56.

23. Although the idea of "the good savage" can be found before Rousseau's time, and despite his giving new expression to it, the widespread opinion established in the late fifteenth century of Indians as living in barbarism still held sway. See Olive P. Dickason's *The Myth of the Savage*, especially chapter X, "Amerindians in Europe."

Engraving of John Dunn Hunter from the 1824 London edition
of *Memoirs of a Captivity*. Author's collection.

were stupid and lazy."[24]

Buffon's absurd notions caught hold among a European readership reaching well beyond mere intellectuals. If his wordsmithery was superior to his science, if his deduction was better than his induction, he nevertheless managed to influence Continental perceptions for years—years even beyond contravening evidence offered to Buffon by Benjamin Franklin and Thomas Jefferson (who sent the naturalist a particularly large stuffed moose).

The collision of the ideas of Rousseau and Buffon helped quite

---

24. Dugatkin, *Mr. Jefferson and the Giant Moose*, xi.

literally set the stage for the appearance of the six Osages, and the question arises whether their tour dispelled either Buffon's degeneracy theory or Rousseau's blind idealism. Human minds being what they are, it would seem that an onlooker's bias could find evidence for one view or the other, no matter that both were preposterously naive and based on theorizing free of true science. Buffon's influence, by the way, might explain Tixier's sentence about Big Soldier's implied boast in his remembering "with particular pleasure that he had married three times"[25] while overseas, an interpretation of "married" the key to his enjoyment.

The final stimulus for the journey was interest stirred in Europe by a book—leaning toward the Rousseauian approach—by American John Dunn Hunter who published his *Memoirs of a Captivity among the Indians of North America from Childhood to the Age of Nineteen* in 1823 in Philadelphia and London, and in the year following in Dresden. Captivity narratives were enormously popular in America from the mid-eighteenth century well into the next, and Hunter's book quickly turned him into a celebrity, especially in England where questions of the authenticity of his narrative (to be distinguished from the accuracy of its details about Indian—especially Osage—life) were not as important as they were to Americans who widely considered him an impostor. Seeing the fascination of discontented Europeans who might conjure up freedoms civilization had lost, in 1827 Delaunay could visualize economic gain from an overseas Osage tour. While there are numerous accounts of American Indians visiting—and being exhibited in—England during the late eighteenth and early nineteenth centuries, across the Channel things were different. From the French Revolution in 1789 and continuing until the restoration of the monarchy in 1816, France was in turmoil, perhaps explaining the absence of records about Indians there until the arrival of the six Osages in 1827. Hunter's book came to the fore in France following a long review of it written in 1824 by Nicolas Perrin for the influential periodical *Journal des Voyages*.

To read about the curious mobs that thronged every appearance

---

25. Tixier, *Tixier's Travels*, 99.

of the Osages early in their tour—the daily news accounts, the rings and baubles given Sacred Sun and Hawk Woman, the men smoking fine cigars—is to imagine the glow of an Osage triumph reaching its zenith in the pomp and extravagance of their reception by the king of France in his residence. For six *primitifs* who had begun their voyage as deck passengers on a muddy Mississippi River steamboat to be received by the monarch of one of the most powerful countries in the world was a moment unforgettable and nearly unimaginable.

But events beyond the initial glitter of 1827 dimmed progressively and appearances of the Osages in the news grew fewer. By autumn, they had been reduced to begging in the suburbs of Paris and had become victims of exploitation, perhaps not so much by Delaunay as by Europeans. In Paris, hustlers peddled images of the Indians painted on fans, stitched on work bags, cast into metal paperweights, and even baked into spiced-bread figures for hoi polloi to chomp on as they gaped at living warriors who had killed men and taken scalps, and carried off enemy women.

At one point, several young French Lotharios approached Sacred Sun and Hawk Woman, and, with borrowed Osage phrases, attempted to question them about amorous matters. When a man put his arm around the neck of one of the women, Loise asked the bounders to leave. And in Verviers, Belgium, a casino proprietor demanded four of the Osages, including the two women, to sit on chairs atop a billiard table and be ogled like exhibits in a freak show. Sacred Sun and Hawk Woman lowered their heads and wept at the forced humiliation. When Big Soldier fell ill in September of 1829 and his recovery was in doubt, there came an offer to buy his corpse for display in a "menagerie, stuffed like the late Hottentot Venus."[26] As the entourage moved through Belgium, Holland, Germany, Switzerland, and Italy—countries where curiosity about them was probably less keen to begin with—interest declined, despite their dance performances and war songs, and so did the price to see them, along with the material perquisites of their celebrity. Exacerbating things, surely, was Delaunay's temporary imprisonment for the 1799 debt

---

26. Quoted in Grant Foreman, "Our Indian Ambassadors," 143.

and his—and apparently Loise's—periodic departures.

Unable to speak anything more than a few words of French, the Osages needed charity to buy their return to native shores; eventually, several patrons proved generous. For unknown reasons, the tour divided itself into two contingents. One group of travelers (Big Soldier, Sacred Sun and her daughter, either Black Bird or Young Soldier—probably the latter—and Paul Loise with his teenage son) went to Paris where they eventually found help from the longtime friend of America, seventy-three-year-old Marquis de Lafayette who took them to his home and helped raise money to send them from Le Havre to Norfolk, Virginia, in November of 1829 aboard the ship *Savannah*. But while on the dock at Le Havre, the possessions the Osages had managed to retain during their travails were seized for travel debts incurred under the name of conductor Loise. Lafayette was able to help settle the obligations and later to return some of their property once they were again in America.

The key Samaritan for the second troupe (Little Chief, Hawk Woman, and Black Bird or Young Soldier) was Bishop William Du Bourg, who had lived in Missouri from 1818 to 1823, when he founded a church in Florissant, today a suburb of St. Louis. He too put out a call for contributions to assist their return, and in Bordeaux in the spring of 1830, the second group of Osage travelers boarded the *Charlemagne* bound for New York City.

If the reports saying Black Bird and Young Soldier both died aboard ship are correct, then it was only Little Chief, Big Soldier, Hawk Woman, and Sacred Sun with her daughter who safely returned to their native villages. Later accounts claim that in the years following, the surviving Osage travelers spoke well of their experience overseas, and until his death in 1844, Big Soldier wore the bronze medallion bearing Lafayette's image the Marquis had given him in Paris.

How the Story Has Come Down

Quite soon after the appearance of *Six Red Indians* and *Remarks on Six Indians*, Paul Vissier came out with his *History*, based in part on the former booklet. Other than McKenney's 1830 sketch of Sacred

Sun, we have found only a few further accounts or significant references to the Osage tour until 1900 when a brief article in the *American Anthropologist* announced the acquisition by the Bureau of American Ethnology of the "two rare pamphlets" that Alice C. Fletcher used to give a much-condensed summary of the trip.

In 1928 Oklahoma historian Grant Foreman, in his "Our Indian Ambassadors to Europe," mentioned a number of nineteenth-century newspaper reports, both in Europe—especially France—and in the United States, in which New Orleans and St. Louis newspapers took a special interest in the journey. In 1943 his wife Carolyn Foreman expanded the story in her *Indians Abroad.* The work of the Foremans, despite a few inaccuracies, has been the most complete to date, but they do not consider the import of several key 1827 documents now included or referenced here. Further, a reader who compares our version of events with the Foremans' interpretation—who both accept McKenney's opinions—will find here a somewhat different story.

The only previous complete translation of *Six Red Indians* is that of Margot Ford McMillen and Pippa Letsky, published in the *Missouri Historical Review* in 2003. In our rendition, we tried to be as literal as is tolerable to a contemporary reader, but the hurried, snip-and-assemble compilations of *Six Red Indians*—and to a lesser extent the *Remarks* and the Vissier booklets—are stylistically ungifted, with sentences tending toward the repetitively telegraphic in length and structure, and too often haphazardly linked by semicolons. Nevertheless, only when phrasings go beyond reasonable forbearance do we try to ease such infelicities. Believing as we do that misinformation and prepossession shape history as readily as their opposites, in the translations themselves we avoided correcting every interpretative error and each distortion (sometimes included for no reason other than embellishment) or bias, and we rectified in the footnotes only the more egregious ones. Vissier employs the term "history" loosely; what appears in his work and in *Six Red Indians* might be more accurately termed folk ethnography, some of it generalized from other tribes. Reading the texts, a reader should continually consider the limited knowledge each of the three authors had of Native life in North America and see these works as expressive of a deep desire of three French people to comprehend and appreciate something of Native North America, and particularly a people closely linked to France for more than a century. The booklets present a telling picture of two cultures from different hemispheres and dissimilar comprehensions meeting in a rising, technological civilization, each trying to make sense of the other during a massive reordering of society.

———————

Today the epicenter of the Children of the Middle Waters is in Osage County, Oklahoma, with an official tribal enrollment of about ten thousand people. To lend a detail of historical perspective, we will mention that after the nineteenth-century dispersal from their native Missouri homelands, the Osage tribe in the twentieth century became beneficiaries of immense reserves of oil and gas under their new land in Indian Territory, now Oklahoma, once thought to be almost worthless. From these previously unknown resources, the Osages became for a while one of the wealthiest cultural groups on the planet. Seeing opportunity for easy money, whites, ironically, began conniving ways to become Osages and include themselves on the official tribal roll. Perhaps, to take a longer view of Osage history, William Clark's treaties did not, when all is said and done, damn him in the hereafter.

A Note on Illustrations

A DOZEN ILLUSTRATIONS of the six Osages who traveled to Europe in 1827 are known to have survived. The earliest are two physiognotrace portraits—one of Little Chief, the other of Big Soldier—drawn in 1804 in Washington by the celebrated artist Charles de Saint-Mémin, who labeled the former image Cashunghia, the artist's try at representing the complex Osage name. The physiognotrace was a device allowing an artist to achieve a remarkably precise outline of a human profile, which then would be filled in with details and tone to create portraits that can excel in accuracy compared to other methods of rendition for that time. Saint-Mémin's depiction of Little Chief can be readily compared with the painting of him by Louis-Léopold Boilly two decades later.

Of the five known editions of *Six Red Indians*, four are illustrated. All images are lithographs, a relatively new printing technique; a random few of them were hand colored. The image in the two Paris editions is a sketch done in near caricature by Guillaume-François Colson and shows what may be Little Chief addressing the other Osages. The Brussels printing also contains the Colson image, although redrawn and reduced to the size of an index card. Of all versions of *Six Red Indians*, that from Leipzig has the largest image—a tri-fold, eight-by-ten-inch lithograph based on a drawing by Luther Brand; it depicts the Osages seated in the Theater des Arts in Rouen.

In the artistically finest picture of the Osages rendered while they were in Europe, Louis-Léopold Boilly, a highly regarded artist of the time, depicted Hawk Woman, Little Chief, and Young Soldier in a montage. We have not located the original source of the lithograph, but we suspect Boilly created it to be sold independently to capitalize on the keen interest shown early in the Osage visit.

Upon their return to the United States in 1830, the important early nineteenth-century portraitist of North American Indians, Charles Bird King, painted Mohongo holding her daughter. Perhaps the most well-known of all the portrayals, this work accompanied Thomas McKenney's biographical sketch of her and became part of his *The Indian Tribes of North America*. The original oil-on-panel painting (seventeen by fourteen inches) was lost in the great Smithsonian fire of 1865, leaving only the lithograph published in the book and an apparent replica painting now in private hands. King received twenty dollars for the initial double portrait. Andrew S. Hughes, a sub-agent to various tribes, who accompanied the four surviving Osages on their return home, wrote to McKenney: "The extraordinary harmony and fine expression of Mo-hon-go's face and the speaking expression of her child are suspected by some to be artificial. I declare . . . that I think it is not within the power of any artist to put on canvas a likeness of any human being more perfect or more life-like than are both Mo-hon-go and her child" (Biddle, *Recommendatory Notices*, p. 8).

Four years later, George Catlin painted Little Chief at Fort Gibson in Indian Territory (Oklahoma) in two versions, a watercolor sketch and an oil. In 1843, at a huge council held in Tahlequah, Indian Territory, the renowned John Mix Stanley spent a week with Big Soldier and painted his portrait, thereby creating a kind of bookend closure to all the portrayals that began about 1804 with the remarkable visages of Big Soldier and Little Chief.

Of the tour leaders—Delaunay, Tesson, and Loise—we have found a likeness of only the latter; it is an 1806 silhouette by Charles Willson Peale, another celebrated artist of the time.

That so many images of this small group were created by renowned artists here and in Europe is as attributable to the importance of the Osage tribe in the early nineteenth century as it is to the travelers' distinctive physiognomies that seemed to fulfill the expectations of white imaginations. These are faces one does not readily come upon today, even in Osage County, Oklahoma, the tribal heartland. All of these images, but for the one by John Mix Stanley, are included in *An Osage Journey to Europe, 1827–1830*.

Guillaume-François Colson's illustration for the third and fourth editions of *Six Red Indians*. The State Historical Society of Missouri.

Luther Brand's tri-fold illustration, "The Indians from the Tribe of the Osage, who are still in Paris—[here] at the theater in Rouen," for the Leipzig Edition of *Six Red Indians*.

Louis-Léopold Boilly's montage portrait of (*clockwise*) Hawk Woman, Little Chief, and Young Soldier. Probably produced independently of a booklet and sold as an individual print. The State Historical Society of Missouri.

Charles Bird King's 1830 oil portrait of Sacred Sun (Mohongo) from
Thomas McKenney's and James Hall's *The Indian Tribes of North
America*. The State Historical Society of Missouri.

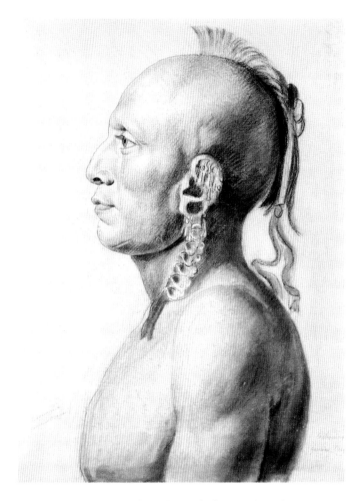

Charles Balthazar Julien Fevret de Saint-Mémin's ca. 1804
physiognotrace of Little Chief (Cahshunghia). Collection of The New-
York Historical Society, object no. 1860.90.

Charles Balthazar Julien Fevret de Saint-Mémin's ca. 1805 unidentified
physiognotrace, likely of Big Soldier, probably made in Washington,
D.C. Collection of The New-York Historical Society, object no. 1860.94.

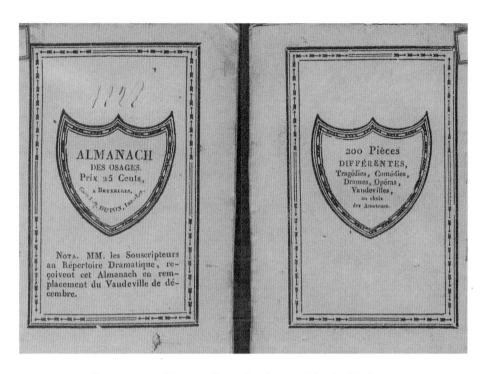

Paper cover of the 1827 Brussels edition of *Six Red Indians*.
Author's collection.

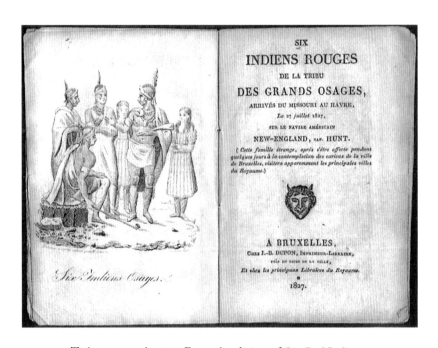

Title page to the 1827 Brussels edition of *Six Red Indians*.
Author's collection.

About the Text of

Six Red Indians

A HALF-DOZEN EDITIONS of *Six Red Indians* appeared in 1827 and apparently none thereafter. We have examined five of the six— the one published in Le Havre, two in Paris, one in Brussels, and one in Leipzig—but we have not been able to locate anything that could be a first edition. That initial printing, appearing within hours of the arrival of the Osages in Le Havre, may have been little more than a mere announcement or news account. If that should be so, then Father Matthew Anduze might have had a hand in calling attention to relevant cultural material, especially Nicolas Perrin's review of John Dunn Hunter's *Memoirs of a Captivity*, published in London only three years earlier. Whatever the content or whoever the author of that original edition, we think it likely David Delaunay, as leader of the Osage tour, underwrote its publication. The first printing may have been small, just enough to gauge French interest in the Indians, but sales were apparently sufficient to exhaust the supply and warrant a "revised, corrected, and augmented" second edition no later than four days after the Osages landed.

This version contains two revealing details unremarked until now: On the verso of the title page is, effectively, a statement of copyright:

> We, the undersigned, in charge of the management of the Six Osage Indians, certify that the information given here, printed by M. S. Faure, in Le Havre, was written up based on documents furnished by our Interpreter, who has spent a great number of years among the Indians; that all the details which it contains are the exact truth, and that the Author of this work, and Editor, is

the only one who has the right to publish it, not wanting, we the undersigned, to concede this right to any other person.

Le Havre, August 1st, 1827

D. DELAUNAY, F. C. TESSON,
Directors of Management
Paul LOISE, Interpreter.

The problem here lies in the punctuation and syntax of this sentence: Is the "Author" one and the same as the "Editor," as the singular verb that follows suggests? If so, that person must be David Delaunay. And what documents did Loise provide? Could that man of the backcountry have had enough literacy to know about Perrin's long review? Perhaps Loise did little more than turn over material given him by Father Anduze, whom the Osages had asked in New Orleans to prepare the way for their arrival. To create *Six Red Indians*, Delaunay then could have cobbled together items around Perrin's review of *Memoirs of a Captivity* and perhaps also included comments based on Loise's firsthand knowledge of Osage life. The second edition, although described as "revised, corrected, and augmented," contains no information on the Indians while they were in Le Havre, other than remarks about their arrival. This is the version Paul Vissier cites and belittles in his *History of the Tribe of the Osages*.

The third and fourth editions, both published in Paris, are virtually identical in content and format: They are duodecimos (five by seven and three-quarter inches). The third edition appeared around the tenth of August and updates the title-page description to "Revised, corrected, and augmented with interesting details of their sojourn in Le Havre." The fourth version came out two weeks later.

The Brussels edition appeared in a reduced format of a sexto-decimo (three by five and one-half inches) and is clearly based on those of Paris, although for some reason it omits three paragraphs about Osage religion. One Brussels copy we examined was in thin, lime-green paper covers with a strange title, "Almanach des Osages," although the almanac is nothing more than a four-page table of saints' days for 1828. The wrapper indicates the pamphlet was distributed free to the audience of a December 1827 vaudeville show, presumably the onstage appearance of the Osages singing and dancing. The title page notes: "This foreign family, after having offered themselves to the contemplation of inquisitive people in Brussels, will apparently go to the principal cities of the Kingdom."

The Leipzig version, *Die Sechs Kupferrothen Indianer* [*The Six Copper-Red Indians*], states that the German translation is based on the third French edition, and it does, in fact, follow that text closely but for two exceptions: It deletes a paragraph about French place-names along the Missouri River, and in the conclusion it mentions the visit of the Osages to the king of France on August 21, adding that the Indians were still in Paris. This edition includes a foldout illustration by Luther Brand that is superior to any illustration in the French-language versions of *Six Red Indians*.

All copies we have seen were originally published in flimsy paper covers typical of the time, scarce protection for the pages within over the intervening years. Whatever the case, *Six Red Indians* is relatively difficult to find, even in major libraries.

The half-title page of the various French editions, imprinted in capital letters with Les Indiens Osages, has led some modern commentators to refer to the work as *The Osage Indians*, an error that Paul Vissier compounds by calling the pamphlet *Des Indiens Osages* [*About the Osage Indians*]. These incorrect designations can derail a title search alone for the booklet.

For reasons of its generally superior completeness, we have chosen to translate and annotate the third edition, which also appears to be the one with the widest circulation. The endnotes document differences among the five known printings.

SIX

RED INDIANS

FROM THE TRIBE

OF THE GREAT OSAGE,

ARRIVED FROM MISSOURI AT LE HAVRE,

THE 27TH OF JULY 1827,

ON THE AMERICAN SHIP

NEW-ENGLAND, CAPTAIN HUNT.

THIRD EDITION

REVISED, CORRECTED, AND AUGMENTED WITH INTERESTING DETAILS
ABOUT THEIR SOJOURN IN LE HAVRE

PARIS.

DELAUNAY, BOOKSELLER

TO HER ROYAL HIGHNESS MADAME THE DUCHESS OF ORLEANS

PALAIS-ROYALE, NO. 243

1827

Six Red Indians

The Osage Indians
Course of the Missouri River

THE ACQUISITION OF LOUISIANA by the government of the United States which bought this immense country in 1803 from the residents to whose domination it was subjected, and by its subsequent treaties made with Indians, have rendered the American Union master of a vast region watered by the Missouri River.[1] The concessions obtained from the savage natives cost the present owners very little—portions of the territory one-hundred-thousand arpents in size being transferred for less than two hundred dollars.[2]

The Missouri is a river with its source near the Rocky Mountains, not far from the divisions separating North America from the Columbia of the North. The mouth of the Missouri is at Fort Saint Louis[3] where it mingles with the Mississippi which waters Louisiana and New Orleans and empties into the sea forty-five leagues from this latter city.

---

1. The tribe, during the time of French influence, lived principally in two villages, the larger group (the Great Osage) on the lower Osage River in Missouri and a smaller band (the Little Osage) on the Missouri River not far away. Big Chief was attached to the latter group.

2. The 1803 purchase of the Louisiana Territory, some 828,000 square miles, works out to about three pennies an acre, although figuring the total cost per acre is difficult because of other considerations such as interest. On a trip to Washington to visit the President in July of 1804, the Osage delegation heard from Thomas Jefferson, "We have no views upon [your people] but to carry on a commerce useful to them and us" (Jackson, *Letters of the Lewis and Clark Expedition*, Vol. 1, 202). Four years later the tribe was pressured to cede—"fer a verry Small Sum" (quoted by Holmberg, *Dear Brother: Letters of William Clark*, 154), in William Clark's words—an area amounting to nearly half of present-day Missouri and a good portion of Arkansas. An arpent, equal to about one acre, was a unit of French measurement in use until the middle of the nineteenth century.

3. The Spanish first fortified the settlement on the Mississippi River in 1780, but by 1827 the defenses were in disarray to the degree that the town could

The course of the Missouri is majestic, and a short while ago some intrepid American engineers traveled on it with unheard-of effort by means of steamboats,[4] which were broken down into parts and transported on beasts of burden when impassable passages were encountered. An infinitude of smaller rivers carry the tribute of their waters to the Missouri; among these is the Grand Osage which waters the territory of the people from whom six members have just disembarked at Le Havre. The Missouri receives this river forty-three leagues from Fort St. Louis.[5]

Memories of the French

At one hundred leagues upriver towards its source are the last French fortifications,[6] abandoned like all the others; the only imperishable monuments we have left there are the names we gave to places, prairies, and rivers which they retained while changing masters: One still finds[7] la Bonne Femme, la Prune, le Mont-Brun, les Charbonniers, la Terre-Blanche, etc.

(*cont.*) hardly be considered a fort. The confluence of the Missouri and Mississippi rivers is seventeen miles north of the old town center.

4. The steamboat referred to is probably the *Western Engineer,* built in Pittsburgh for Major Stephen Long's 1819 expedition to reach the headwaters of the Missouri River. The *Engineer* made it upstream as far as what is now Council Bluffs, Iowa, a distance today of 616 miles. See the *Missouri Gazette*, November 13, 1818.

5. The nautical measurement of a league can vary from about two and a half miles to nearly five miles. Today, in the engineered and shortened Missouri, the mouth of the Osage River is 130 miles from the Missouri-Mississippi confluence.

6. Fort Orleans was established by France in 1723 above the juncture of the Grand and Missouri rivers in what is now Carroll County, Missouri. Its exact location has not been discovered.

7. Of these particular French place-names, only la Bonne Femme ("the Good Woman," called so by Lewis and Clark) has retained its original appellation. Two different creeks flowing into the Missouri about twenty-eight miles from each other in adjoining Missouri counties—Boone and Howard—now carry that name.

Names of Peoples Neighboring the Osages

The shores of the Missouri are peopled with a plentitude of Indian tribes, the complete denomination of which has no place here; counting only the red nations, we have the Osages of whom we will especially speak, the Kanzas, the Pawnee-Loups, the Republican Pawnees, the Grand Pawnees, the Poncas, Omahas, Comanches, the Plais or Bald-heads, the Utes, Sauks, Fox, Ioways, and Sioux;[8] the latter tribe is much larger than the others.

Love of the Savages for Their Region

The mores of these peoples, some of whom call the President of the United States their father, present as a whole the same characteristic traits. It's only in the details that one notices nuances. Habits are modified according to the location of the places where they dwell, and their physiognomy changes—if you compare the Indian of the

---

8. The French text lists the tribes as: les Konzas, les Pawni-Loups, les Pawni-Republicains, Grands-Pawnis, les Puncas, Omawhas, Pandoucas, les Plais ou têtes chauves, les Jetans, les Sanks [*sic*], les Renards, les Jovays, et les Sioux. The second edition of *Six Red Indians* has "La Plais" rather than "les Plais," an indication the list was taken from Edwin James's *Account of an Expedition from Pittsburgh to the Rocky Mountains*, published in 1823. James gives the tribes as "Osages, Konzas, Pawnee Loups, Pawnee Republicans, Grand Pawnees, Puncas, Omawhas, and Sioux, Padoucas, La Plais or Bald Heads, Ietans, Sauks, Foxes and Ioways." James may have drawn his list from William Clark's "Statistical View" (reprinted in Moulton's edition of the Lewis and Clark *Journals*). Clark mentions "la Plays" or "La Playes" as a wandering tribe principally on the plains around the sources of the Arkansas and Red rivers. The Padoucas, La Plais, and Ietans are all considered bands of the Alitan (also Aliatan) or Snake Indians. Vissier deletes this name in his list. "Sioux," then as now, is a careless, yet popular, term that lumps together several related but separate tribes. The Osage language is mutually intelligible to a greater or lesser degree to the so-called "Sioux" peoples of the Upper Missouri River.

Plains with the Indian of the [Rocky] Mountains, the savage of the forests and the one who built his hut on the bank of a river; but the tenacity of these men for the place where they were born is the same everywhere; it is a passion rivaled only by their ardent love for independence and liberty, attributes so precious they would not exchange the slightest part for the benefits of civilization. Their favorite maxim is that anyone can do whatever he wants if he harms not another, but one doesn't progress in civilization with that rule of conduct. No people, says Mr. Hunter,[9] have a stronger attachment to their land, and death holds no horror for an Indian if his country can gain some advantage from his demise. Self-interest is never taken into consideration. The savage submits to his destiny, fully persuaded he is doing his duty, with a magnanimity that ordinary souls are incapable of

---

9. In 1823 in Philadelphia, John Dunn Hunter published his *Manners and Customs of Several Indian Tribes Located West of the Mississippi*. The following year, three augmented editions came out in London, re-titled *Memoirs of a Captivity among the Indians of North America from Childhood to the Age of Nineteen with Anecdotes Descriptive of Their Manners and Customs.* Hunter's book, via Nicolas Perrin's 1824 review of it in *Journal des Voyages,* is the primary source for much of the material published in *Six Red Indians,* as it is for Vissier's *History.* For a comparison of source and variation, here is the relevant passage from the English edition:

> No people are more enthusiastically attached to their country, than the Indians. This does not originate, in any considerable degree from those local circumstances which influence the feelings in civilized life, but from the love of national distinction and glory. Each nation is divided into families, or sub-tribes, which are taught to become competitors for the meed of excellence, in whatever relates to their mode of life; and this honorable strife exists among all members of their respective families. But it, together with ambition and self love, is strenuously cultivated as subservient to national attachment and devotion. It is this which constitutes their union and strength; and, to an Indian, when his country is to be benefited by it, death has no terrors; self is never taken into the account; and he submits to his fate, under the impression that he has done his duty, with a magnanimity not to be appreciated by worldly minds. (328)

appreciating. Skilled at concealing the emotions he feels, he never forgets a favor or an insult.

Habitations

The Indians live in huts that in their language they call "wigwams." A few tree trunks brought together without being joined form the walls of these crude structures. Smoke escapes from an opening made in the roof. A chimney would be a luxury. Their beds are made from two planks trimmed with an axe, upon which they place a bear skin or bison skin in the winter; in the summer, they use moss found growing in the swamps. These men of nature do not bother themselves with anything except what is necessary to keep from dying of hunger or cold; everything beyond those limits is considered superfluous, and they renounce it. Liberty and weakness have never walked side by side. Furnishings are unknown. Their cooking equipment would not surpass that of our lower Breton peasants:[10] a bowl or hollow scraped into a piece of maple wood; two or three plates made of crude sun-dried pottery, some wooden forks—those are all the furnishings of a hut. Certain tribes are somewhat better equipped, having iron pots and clay dishes in shapes not unattractive, but such wares are few.

———

(*cont.*) In *Six Red Indians*, material originating with Hunter comes not directly from his *Memoirs* but from Perrin's review. Here, in translation, is Perrin's version of the same passage:

> No people have a stronger attachment to their country. Death holds no horror for an Indian, says Mr. Hunter, if his country can gain some advantage from his demise. One's self-interest is never taken into consideration. The Savage submits to his destiny, fully persuaded he is doing his duty, with a magnanimity which ordinary souls are incapable of appreciating. (98)

Beyond referring twice to Hunter by name and as "an American traveler," "a young stranger," and "a modern-day traveler," *Six Red Indians* gives no other information about him or his book.

See note 28 for Vissier's *History*.

10. Bretons, especially those living near the remote southwest coast, were considered by nineteenth-century Parisians to be almost uncivilized.

Food

Most of these Indians are hunters and fishermen, and their food is scarcely more refined than their clothes; they live on roots, fish, and buffalo flesh half-roasted and boiled,[11] to which they add in the spring the bark of a shrub[12] with a sweet taste something like the turnip in Europe. One unusual dish, which probably only a few people could get used to, is a soup made with ants plentiful in the region.[13] The Snake Indians[14] are especially fond of it and never fail to serve this soup at family reunions or celebrations.

Women

The further customs are separated from civilization, the less women are treated with the consideration necessary to a sex nature did not endow with strength for the work people in savage lands think they

---

11. The second edition reads "roasted or boiled," which seems more likely.

12. This may refer to the sassafras and the bark on its root, used by Native peoples for sundry medicinal and culinary purposes. In 1574, Frenchman Nicholas Menardes wrote in his *Joyfull Newes Out of the New Founde Worlde* (in translation) that sassafras "dooeth make fatte [and] doth cause lust to meate" (quoted in Donald Culross Peattie's *A Natural History of Trees of Eastern and Central North America*, 294). White settlers in later years decocted sassafras root into a spring tonic, but the comparison with a turnip suggests a tuber rather than bark. If so, the reference might be to the Indian turnip (one of many names for *Psoralea esculenta*), an important food for Plains Indians. Francis La Flesche, however, in his *The Osage Tribe: Rite of the Chiefs*, does not mention *P. esculenta* as a principal tuber used by the Osages; rather, he names Indian potato or broadleaf arrowhead (*Sagittaria latifolia*), American lotus (*Nelumbo lutea*), groundnut (*Glycine apios*, currently *Apios americana*), and hog peanut (*Falcata comosa*, currently *Amphicarpaea bracteata*). See Meriwether Lewis's lengthy description of *esculenta*—"the white apple"—he encountered on the western expedition in his journal entry for May 8th, 1805 (Moulton, Vol. 4, 125–26).

13. Vissier repeats this dubious statement and tries to enhance its validity by assuming he knows the very species of ant in question. See note 22 in his *History*.

14. A name enemies of the Shoshones applied to them. The French text has this as "les Indiens Snathe," surely a typographical error.

have the right to require of them. The unfortunate Indian women, of all females in the world, have the most right to complain about the abuse of marital power. Savage women do not have the least bit of coquetry, although they really enjoy daubing their face with vermilion.[15] One can hardly conceive that females who have such a mild appearance can be so frightening and so cruel when they fall upon an enemy prisoner.

Agriculture and routine work of every sort are among their tasks. Men would think themselves degraded by doing it; they live in continual indolence. They rarely deign to go out to make weapons or build canoes or wigwams, but even in the latter two projects, men make women help them. When different tribes go to hunting lands, the male savage walks proudly carrying only his bow and gun. On the other hand, the woman serves as a beast of burden as she carries on her shoulders, with the help of a strap across her forehead, all the equipment for the family, never receiving—if she succumbs to the load—either help or signs of compassion from her spouse. Once arrived at the place where the camp is to be established, the man reposes while the woman puts down her burden and busies herself setting up the tent and preparing a meal.

If the male goes hunting,[16] he almost always returns without carrying back his prey. He goes into his hut and stretches out on the moss, his wife takes off his *mitas* and his *mokosins* (leggings and shoes), and she washes his feet, fills his pipe, and awaits his orders. "My kill is at such and such a distance," the savage tells her; the woman leaves quickly; and it is remarkable that in these immense, empty lands, the unfortunate savage woman never goes astray, but returns carrying the game. Thus this liberty the Indians are so jealous of really profits only the men. Women are excluded from it. They are slaves! If such is the law of nature, you must agree that nature gave a very large portion to the masculine sex.

---

15. A pigment made from mercuric sulfide. The Colson illustration of the Osages seems to be the best match to the description of the appearance of the Osages while in France.

16. Vissier refers scornfully to this passage in his chapter 8.

Children

Maternal care is not as all-encompassing in their country as in civilized lands. Women employed in rough work do not take much care of their off-spring. When a child is born, it is attached by thongs to a plank covered with vegetable fiber, and the mother hangs it on a tree while she goes about her domestic affairs. The anguish of these little creatures lasts up to ten months before they gain freedom of their limbs; then the children can crawl or drag themselves on the ground if their legs are not strong enough to hold them upright. Boys go naked; girls are dressed in a shirt which covers them to the waist and a very short sort of skirt which comes half-way down their legs. Children are nursed until age two or three, a custom attributed to the difficulty of finding, for such young beings, food suitable to the weakness of their organs.

Clothing

The ordinary dress of women differs little from children of their same sex. They both circle the head with a leather band or a ribbon of some cloth decorated with glass beads, medallions, or feathers of divers colors. Men wear no garment except a strip of cloth large enough to cover their loins; they throw a bear skin, buffalo skin, or perhaps a wool blanket over their shoulders to form a drapery the ends of which they hold in one hand. They have buskins of soft fur and quite appropriate for running. When they walk about their wig-wams, they are armed with a large knife, and they carry a long-stemmed pipe because they are heavy smokers, a habit they got from the Spanish. Young men go naked even during the most intense cold spells, and leave the wearing of furs to the older men who would make fun of a young man taking on such airs of a sybarite.

Lesser Sioux or Osage chiefs having pretensions of refinement or elegance shave their heads, leaving only a tuft of hair on the crown which they carefully decorate with little slips of silver, ivory, ebony, or feathers. Each tribe has its own color, its favorite hue; some paint their faces yellow with roucou[17] while others prefer red with black

---

17. Perhaps the pigment made from the anatta plant; also known as rocou.

ornamentation. A mixture of the last two tints is the ne plus ultra of good taste; one cannot refuse anything to a young man who paints his cheeks with rings, crescents, arrows, and designs most bizarre.

To add even more to their beauty, the *fashionables* separate their ears from their heads with a knife to the extent that the ears are held in place only at the extremities; then brass wires are inserted, one on top of another, into the slits which, because of the weight, cause the ear to hang to the shoulder. Nostrils undergo similar mutilation and are filled with different kinds of pendants. So there you have men of nature who refuse to submit to the yoke of civilization, but who submit themselves to customs more tyrannical than anyone might imagine. It is true that man is evident in everything man does, whether you find him in the center of Paris, Peking, or on the wild shores of the Missouri. The men wrap the ankles of their feet with little lanyards to which are attached metal platelets that hit against each other and make a tiny ringing noise that pleases the Indian when running or dancing, activities he is very fond of.

Hunting

All Indians are great hunters, their weapons being the bow and the carbine; a buffalo, bison,[18] beaver, or bear, hunted by them, rarely escapes their dexterity. The force of an arrow shot by one of these savage is truly extraordinary: People have seen an arrow go through the body of a buffalo and fall to the ground on the opposite side of the animal, sometimes even carrying some distance beyond. American agents travel among the tribes at certain times, gaining for a very low price—either in money or an exchange of goods—the product of hunts of people especially involved in this occupation. Indians

---

18. The French text uses both terms, *buffle* and *bison*. We follow that pattern without trying to fathom the writer's distinction, but note that early French descriptions of North American fauna often used *buffle* for any large game animal. "Buffalo" is a common, if incorrect, term for the North American bovine, *Bison bison*; true buffaloes are native to the Old World. Nevertheless, in our translation, *buffle* is always given as "buffalo" while *bison* remains "bison."

strongly insist[19] on the right to the game within their own territory, but they are nonetheless ready to poach on the land of neighbors. Game is the cause of almost all quarrels arising between the chiefs and among their inferiors.

War

The variety and abundance of game, the spontaneous growth of edible plants, the mildness of the climate, and the ease with which inhabitants find everything there to satisfy their needs, makes control of land the cause of continual war among tribes,[20] and those battles incessantly waged against one another, which keep them in a fighting mood, have, until now, made efforts to civilize them all but useless. Their arms are tomahawks, clubs, knives, arrows, and poor guns.

Prisoners are well guarded but not mistreated unless the enemy is chasing those who took them captive, in which case the captured are immediately put to death. Wounded men undergo the same fate, later being mutilated—even cut into pieces—either by the victors or by their women who, if they happen upon cadavers, cut off the limbs which they fasten to ropes and drag here and there, all the while shouting cries of joy as horrible for the sound as for its cause.

In each village one encounters slender poles, eighteen to twenty feet long and painted red, stuck into the ground or more often attached to the roofs of houses: These poles carry remains of human skulls with hair wafting in the wind.

Human skulls, those terrible proofs of the barbarism of Indians, are for them of great worth and hang as trophies and ornaments in their wigwams. According to the status of the unfortunate beings whose skulls they once were, new names or titles of honor are awarded to the victors in periodic solemnities. The young warrior then believes himself well rewarded for the dangers and fatigues of his campaigns.

---

19. This sentence and the following one are taken verbatim from Perrin's review of John Dunn Hunter's *Memoirs of a Captivity*.

20. Directly from Perrin.

Religion

As best as Mr. Hunter, an American traveler,[21] was able to determine, he believes all Indians are theists. In conformity with their traditions, they have from time immemorial worshiped a single God, the Great Spirit, the only supreme and intelligent Being who created and governs all things. Consequently, it would not be extraordinary to find among the savages a system of pure and incorruptible theocracy; but, [in his text] a few pages further on, Mr. Hunter dispels this idea by telling us that when Indians are in great affliction, they with equal fervor address prayers to the Evil Spirit which, although inferior to the Good Spirit, has sufficient power and is constantly busy looking for ways to torment mankind. By the word *spirit*, they mean a being which, having the capacity to manifest itself, nevertheless remains invisible. The Great Spirit according to them has a corporeal form and a most excellent and eternal nature not susceptible to any change. They also have some variable notions about agents—subordinate to the two great powers of good and evil—which invisibly attach themselves to mortals and influence their actions, and in ordinary cases are distributors of punishments and rewards. Belief in a future existence and an accounting for one's own actions is, if not universal, at least rather general among them; but their having no conception of the soul or intellectual pleasure, this idea for them is associated with physical objects. After death they expect to go inhabit forever, as a human, a delightful place where they will rejoice in an eternal springtime under a cloudless sky, a land where they will find abundant game.

They say they have never seen the master of life, and consequently are unable to personify him, but they have often heard his voice mixed in with claps of thunder.

Maxims

Never steal, say the chiefs, except from your enemy to whom it is

---

21. The first paragraph is verbatim from Perrin, with the exception of the added phrase "an American traveler."

rightful to do harm in any possible way. When you become a man, be adroit and brave in battle and defend your hunting lands from any infringement. Never let squaws and children lack for anything. Protect squaws and strangers from all insults. Never deceive friends in any way. Be sensitive to insults. Take revenge on enemies. Drink not the white man's poisoned strong-water (spirits) for it comes from the Evil One to cause the downfall of Indians. Fear not death—it is a cause of fear only for cowards. Obey your elders—especially your kin—and respect them. Fear the Evil One and conciliate him so he does you no harm. Love and worship the Great Spirit who created us all, gave us lands filled with game, and protects our lives.[22]

Agriculture

Because food for these Indians is based primarily on the products of hunting, they have made up to the present very little progress in agriculture; but they do grow wheat, tobacco, pumpkins, and corn, and they weed and water their fields in dry seasons.[23]

Their progress in manufacturing has been more pronounced, far out-distancing the Americans of the United States in the art of preparing furs and leather. They demonstrate much industry in making pottery, such as pipes, cups, etc. Their canoes,[24] constructed from birch bark or cottonwood, are admired for buoyancy; they know how to carry them along when traveling on land, and they will used as shelter from rain. Independently of the lodges or cabins for families, Indians construct even larger public structures: octagonal, oblong, or square, and sometimes pyramidal. These constructions serve as depositories for public records[25] and objects belonging to the tribe as

------

22. This section is verbatim from Perrin.

23. This section is verbatim from Perrin. Incidentally, the Osage did not raise wheat. See the chapter on "Marriages."

24. While Indians of the north made canoes from birch bark, it was not the material of Osage vessels. Their common craft, the dugout made from cottonwood, was a comparatively heavy and clumsy thing and not nearly as portable as a bark canoe.

25. The Osages had no such facility; this misstatement (as elsewhere) may result from generalizing from practices of other tribes.

a whole. Individuals do not have the right to enter such places except during public ceremonies, and even enemies, if they were capable of getting into them and destroying them, would consider it sacrilegious to disturb them.

Commerce

There are two types of hunting: one for food and one for trade, the latter undertaken by the savages to procure powder, lead, blankets, and vermilion, all traded for hides of buffalo, bear, beaver, and muskrat. One young stranger,[26] while abandoned in the midst of the Osages, had several occasions to see white merchants coming to exchange rifles for hides and furs. When he grew older, he had a strong desire to learn about the people he evidently belonged to by race; but every time he raised the issue, the Indians responded that whites were inferior beings, ungodly, traitors, cowards, and good only for the routine occupations of life.

Marriages

However strong an attachment a young man may have for a woman of his nation, he will not let it be known until he has acquired a reputation as a warrior or a hunter; before this time, if he dares confess the feelings he has, he can count on a refusal and becomes an object of derision from the warriors and of scorn from the squaws. On the other hand, he who has distinguished himself on the field of battle, or earned a reputation as a hunter, becomes the object of advances from young women who attach much honor to a liaison with such an honored man. It often happens that the same individual finds himself obligated to share his favors with several attractive pretenders who become part of a new family and fulfill their respective duties in great harmony.

After the death of her spouse, the haste of a woman to remarry

---

26. Directly from Perrin. This is the first of three unspecific references to John Dunn Hunter. It's unclear why he goes unnamed both here and later, unless perhaps to diminish awareness of the author's heavy reliance on a single printed source—Perrin's review.

is proof of the esteem she has for the memory of her late husband. When a war party returns from a military campaign, women go to meet it some distance away, and if their husbands perished in the action, they tear at their hair, cut their arms and legs, and attack several distinguished warriors whom they will not leave in peace until the men promise to avenge the death of the one they mourn. Pledges of this sort are considered sacred engagements for marriage and are never violated.

When the preliminaries of a marriage are finished, the family and friends of the two parties are invited to the bride's home to attend the ceremony. On this occasion, the guests having arrived, the young bridegroom takes his intended by the hand, stands in front of all, and candidly confesses his attachment to her, promises to protect her, and to furnish her abundantly with game, and at the same time gives her several large pieces of buffalo, elk, or deer as a pledge for the fulfillment of his vows. For her part, the bride makes a similar statement of attachment, promises to grow wheat and to fulfill all the other duties required by her position, and gives her husband a pledge by offering him a measure of wheat or some other object she agrees to supply for the household. The newlyweds then receive the best wishes from all in attendance, and the remainder of the day and part of the night— or even the whole night—is spent in joy, pleasures, and feasting.

Although polygamy is tolerated, most Indians have only one wife, whom they can get rid of with little difficulty. If a man becomes weary of his squaw, he tells his family he no longer feels friendship for her, and he leaves on a hunting expedition without saying whether or when he will return.[27]

Dancing

Savages all over the world are fond of this kind of activity. Whites, blacks, copper-skinned, reds, Hottentots, Kaffirs, Sioux—all love it passionately. The dances of the Osages and other peoples along the Missouri vary according to circumstance; the dancing is lively and

---

27. This section is directly from Perrin except for minor alterations of punctuation and vocabulary.

graceful when celebrating a happy event for the tribe and grave and serious either prior to or after a battle when it then demonstrates combat. The people dance before going to war, and again upon returning. The dance then becomes an image of what may happen on the battlefield, or a repetition of what did happen—both spectacles frightening to an outsider. Armed with pointed, well-sharpened knives, the dancers risk in the rapidity of their movements piercing their hearts or cutting their throats; if this misfortune never happens, it is thanks to the inconceivable dexterity of those who expose themselves to the danger. The objective of this dance is to represent the way they capture, kill, and scalp their enemies; they mix cries and shouts which would make one think them to be wild, crazy men or demons rather than people performing an inoffensive entertainment.

The dance is usually announced, says an eye-witness, by the sound of vocal and instrumental music, both equally crude. The first instrument is a *gong*, a round barrel with a skin stretched over one end which is beaten with a small stick; the second is a slender stick of hardwood having teeth like a saw, which is rubbed continually and not without effort with a smaller stick in a back-and-forth motion.

Those playing these instruments keep exact time with the singers sitting around them, and other Indians mark time by bending their bodies and moving their arms and legs. Three agile individuals, jumping up, dance a few minutes around the crowd; then the music stops, and the dancers return to their seats while rapidly hitting their mouths with their hands, producing a series of loud and shortened sounds not much different from the barking of a dog.

Young women decorate their heads, arms, and legs with feathers, porcupine quills, and cords made from elk, and execute the most outlandish dances with extraordinary twists and turns.[28]

---

28. The Kaffir people of South Africa are noted for their elaborate social organization and height, and the Hottentots are known for their remarkable phonetic language and diminutive stature. The "gong" mentioned in the second paragraph is clearly a description of a drum and comes from James's *Account*. The final section is from Perrin.

Anthropophagy

We have never heard it said that any of the Indian nations along the Missouri have been accused, even by their enemies, of eating human flesh either by choice or to satisfy some horrible sensuality; only extreme hunger can drive them to do so.[29] Once an Ioway Indian, having killed an Osage, forced some children of the same tribe to eat raw a part of his victim's thigh; a Saint-Pierre Sioux, having dried some flesh of a Chippewa he had killed, served it to several white men who ate it without suspecting anything.

The Calendar

Indians begin their year with the spring equinox. They calculate time from one full moon to another, their months having the same designation the French gave to them in their republican calendar, according to changes found in nature—prairie-time, germination-time, etc.—thus they have the month of planting, the month of the buffalo, the month of snow, etc., all represented in their communications by hieroglyphs such as grains of germinating wheat to indicate the month of planting, and so forth for the other months.[30]

---

29. The first sentence makes clear this section was included more for luridness than for any elucidation of actual Osage life. In his chapter 16, Vissier twists the assertion here to further criticize *Six Red Indians*. The "Saint-Pierre Sioux" probably refers to a group in Minnesota rather than along the Missouri River.

30. This section is verbatim from Perrin. After the Revolution, France replaced the Gregorian calendar with the so-called Republican Calendar which began with the autumn equinox and gave each new month thirty days and a freshly coined name based on appropriate natural phenomena—Thermidor (July–August), Germinal (March–April); the missing five (or six) days were added to the last month, Fructidor (August–September). By the by, the English had fun with the calendar, calling, for example, the winter and spring months Wheezy, Sneezy, Freezy, Slippy, Drippy, Nippy, and so forth.

Languages

Since Indian nations speak different languages rather than dialects of the same language, they are often obliged to make themselves understood to each other by adopting signs of pantomime they use with remarkable skill. It is what we may call a language of diplomacy. The language of the Sacs or the North is spoken by more than fifty tribes.[31] The Mohilien language is the idiom of all the nations of the South.[32] Alphabetical characters being unknown, Indians use hieroglyphic symbols; they inscribe their correspondence and all things that must be remembered on the interior bark of the white birch (*betula papyracea*) or on prepared skins.

Stylets of iron, wood, or stone and brushes made of hair, feathers, or wood fibers are the instruments used to draw or paint the most prominent features of a subject they are trying to convey. The reader's imagination must supply the rest.

Whites

The behavior of some whites who had dealings with the peoples of the Missouri was not conducive to giving the Indians a favorable opinion of white morality; thus, traders today have much trouble erasing the sorry impressions created by their predecessors, and it is rare today for traders to succeed in correcting those early views. Some English merchants, wanting to take to London a young Indian belonging to a tribe neighboring the Osages, lavished him with signs of kindness and affection during their visit.[33] The traders told him whites were more powerful and numerous than Indians and that

---

31. This section is lifted directly from Perrin except for three sentences in the middle of the first paragraph beginning with "It is what we may call" and ending with "nations of the South." Interestingly, these additions introduce erroneous or misleading information.

32. We found no reference to any such "idiom" or language. If "Mohilien" is a typographer's error for either "Mohican" or "Mohegan," then a problem of geography appears: those Algonquin tribes are resident in the northeastern United States, not the South.

33. After the first two sentences, this section is verbatim from Perrin.

whites were brave, generous, and lived in big houses—some of which sailed on the great waters—and that whites fought with enormous cannons that could kill many enemies with a single blow. The young man's curiosity was stimulated by these tales, and he was filled with astonishment. He often expressed the wish to see such things, the desire occupying his thoughts for a long time; but his curiosity was repressed for a while by other Indians who told him once he had grown older, had taken many scalps, and had become a fearsome warrior, then he could go see the whites, because only then would his presence put consternation and fear of death in their hearts.

Mourning

Some Indians from the upper Missouri have signs of mourning as disgusting as they are bizarre: they cut the ligaments and joints of their fingers with the same knife they use for meals, and then, putting between their teeth the parts still hanging together, they detach them by pulling and twisting violently, their teeth serving both as a wedge and a saw for this perverse act.

Civilization

We cannot conclude without recounting the observations of a modern-day traveler[34] on the best means to follow in order to civilize these peoples. Up until a short time ago, those Indians who had the misfortune to have some dealings with whites found in them only the scum and castoffs of the population; brutal men without principles, immoral adventurers who introduced them to evil spirits—whiskey

---

34. First paragraph, except for substitution of "a modern-day traveler" for "our author," is verbatim from Perrin as is the second paragraph, other than minor changes in vocabulary. The "traveler" is Hunter. Paul Wilhelm in his *Travels in North America* wrote:

> Obeying authority of his chiefs and the counsels of his old men, [an Osage] acquires with surprising ease the advantages which accrue to a regulated society, and it would not be easy to find an Indian nation to whom the bonds of social union are as dear and holy as to the Osages.

or rum—and those who did more to corrupt their character than the missionaries have done in half a century to improve it, their work hardly crowned by success. It is a maxim among the Indians never to interrupt whoever might be speaking either by yawning, rising up, or by any other sign of discomfort; thus, young missionaries—noticing the attention and patience of their hearers listening attentively to their long sermons about original sin, its expiation, and the mysteries of their respective beliefs—flattered themselves with having made converts to Christianity. But Indians are generally prejudiced against missionaries, no matter what nation they may come from, and the best sermons rarely touch them. White men tell Indians to be honest although Indians have no prisons, no dungeons for an unfortunate debtor, and no locks on their doors. One must add, however, that it is not exclusively against missionaries that they are prejudiced; rather it is against white men in general, notably against those of the United States.

Remarkably, when whites are led by some circumstance to dwell among Indians, the whites often become inalterably attached to native customs, rarely giving them up afterwards. We have examples of whites who, on becoming older, have broken their ties and abandoned civilized ways to take up those of Indians with whom they have fully adapted themselves.

Specific Details about the Six Indians

The Osage nation,[35] to which belong the six Indians who arrived on the *New-England*, is made up of two tribes of fifteen hundred warriors of the Grand and the Little Osages. They are, in general, handsome men and well-built, although those who are visiting France were not chosen for the beauty of their bodies. According to their long-established tradition, they originated from a snail,[36] which, from the banks of the Osage River where they live, was swept away by a

---

35. This entire section does not appear in the second edition.

36. This myth likely derives from an interpolation by Nicholas Biddle, editor of the so-called "Paul Allen edition," 1814, of the Lewis and Clark journals. See Coues, *History of the Lewis and Clark Expedition*, Vol. I, 12–13.

flood on the Missouri and thrown on to its shores. The warmth of the sun caused the snail to grow into a man who returned to his native territory. A beaver quarreled with him about possession of the land, but all was settled by the man's marriage to the daughter of the beaver. From this union came the tribe. For a long time the Osages respected the lives of the beavers, their maternal relatives. But now that beaver pelts command a high price, the Osages no longer spare them, concentrating their familial affections on snails with no economic value.

The chief of our traveling Indians is thirty-eight years old and taller than his companions; he intends after visiting Paris to see Europe. He is called Kihegashugah or the Little Chief. He is accompanied by his wife and her cousin, Myhangah and Gretomih, both eighteen years old. A second chief named Washingsabba or Black Spirit, thirty-two years old, is under his orders and travels with him. They are accompanied by the big soldier, Marcharthitahtoongah, the oldest of the group at forty-five years old, and the little soldier, Minkchatahooh who is only twenty-two.

The skin of these Indians is coppery-red. The chiefs paint their chins and eyes bright vermilion and their cheeks and ears according to individual taste; they mark their faces with a specific sign to express mourning, peace, war, vengeance, or marriage. Their ears are split and decorated with strings of pearls, an operation performed on infants eight days after they are born. Both the men and women have white and even teeth. The men wear no beard and shave their heads[37] except on the crown where one sees a little tuft of one-half-inch-wide hair, painted red, from which hang two six-inch-long braids tied to a silver bar or a vulture's feather.[38] Women have pretty hair parted on the crown, the separation painted with vermilion; they have large, lively eyes, and altogether their physiognomy is most pleasant. They are short, their manners friendly and polite, and when they find occasion for laughter, they seize upon it—like French women. Their appearance is more refined than the men's, draped as they are from the neck to the

---

37. The Osage warriors were noted for their appearance, which has been strikingly captured by the artists who sketched and painted them during their 1827 journey. Warriors went into battle with even their eyebrows plucked.

38. We are unaware of the Osage using a vulture for adornment in any fashion. An eagle or hawk feather is more likely.

knees with a sort of pleated, lightweight percaline[39] of different shades; another garment of the same sort, but red, hangs below it two or three fingers. They have little boots, or rather slippers, with leggings above them called mitas that reach the knee, and are attached with garters of red cloth embroidered with shells. Women make their own slippers and garters; such footwear is common to both sexes.

Men are naked to the waist, the lower part of the body covered by a wool blanket they never take off even after their death when they are buried in this drapery. Men and women wear necklaces of shells, with a rather large shell suspended in the center. But the chief, in place of a shell, wears a silver medallion, with two bracelets of the same metal on his forearms, his head banded with multicolored silk.

When these Indians go out, three of the chiefs other than the principal of them carry a sort of war hatchet or trophy decorated with bells, ribbons, feathers, and shells; they call it *Ichin-Knatchi*. This and the calumet, a long-stemmed pipe of red stone,[40] are the only objects they carry.

The great-grandfather[41] of the chief of these Indians visited France

---

39. A fine, cotton cloth with a glossy surface. In his *Letters and Notes*, George Catlin wrote in 1834 of the Osages: "This tribe, though living, as they long have, near the borders of the civilized community, have studiously rejected everything of civilized customs; and are uniformly dressed in skins of their own dressing— strictly maintaining their primitive looks and manners, without the slightest appearance of innovations, excepting in the blankets, which have been recently admitted to their use instead of the buffalo robes, which are now getting scarce amongst them" (40).

40. Catlinite, also called pipestone, comes from a single quarry in southwest Minnesota and today is still prized by Indians, who alone are allowed to quarry it.

41. The ancestor of Little Chief who visited France soon after the establishment of Fort Orleans in about 1725 would have arrived during the reign of Louis XV. Various editions of *Six Red Indians* mistakenly (probably printer's errors) identify the king either as Louis XIV or Louis XVI. The Leipzig issue speculates on the mistake in two separate notes: the first remarks that the king should be Louis XIV, while the second points out that no Indian chief visited France during the Revolution under Louis XVI. Vissier seizes on the error in the second edition of *Six Red Indians* to belittle the author. See note 46 to the *History*. Margot McMillen identifies Little Chief's ancestor as Boganielhin in the *Missouri Historical Review*, Vol. XCVII, Number 4.

during the reign of Louis XVI; flattered by the reception he received at court, and in all parts of the kingdom he saw, he told his nation about it when he returned to the shores of the Missouri. Upon hearing this tale, the present chief, while still a child, exclaimed: "And I too, I will visit France, if the master of life permits me to become a man!" When the occasion to execute this project, formed at a very young age, presented itself a few months ago, he begged, through his interpreter, Mr. David Delaunay who was in St. Louis at the time, to find him the means of going to France. The dispositions made and the voyage planned, [Little Chief] said his good-byes to his tribe, promised to return, and set forth. He is a prince of blood. The second chief is reputed to be one of the bravest in the tribe, counting among his glorious trophies the scalps of five enemies he has vanquished. Once in Saint Louis, they found several compatriots who tried to shake their resolve by telling them if they attempted to cross the ocean they would be drowned and eaten by fish, but they took no notice of this prediction. Confident in their guide, they put their destiny in his hands, and the caravan embarked on the Mississippi at Saint Louis aboard the steamboat *Commerce*, five hundred leagues from New Orleans where it arrived safely. They were well received in the capital of Louisiana, and were filled with joy to find Mr. Anduze, an American missionary who had traveled the lands whence they came.

These Indians are deists,[42] worshiping the master of life. Here is a prayer they address to him: "Master of life, I trust you. I ask for your protection in all I want to do. To whom should I turn? To men like myself? No. It is to you, the One Almighty."

While intoning this prayer, beginning at one o'clock in the morning and continuing until daybreak, they look towards the sky, and continue repeating it for five days; then they refrain from praying for

---

42. This paragraph and the following two appear only in the third and fourth editions. The second edition reads: "These Indians are deists; they worship the master of life; every evening they pray to him. Upon entering the harbor at Le Havre, they came out on deck and thanked God for having granted them safe crossing." The Brussels version omits this in its entirety.

the same amount of time. Women recite the prayer before planting corn, and men before going hunting or into battle.

Prior to embarking at New Orleans, the big soldier harangued the sea in these terms: "You, sea, do you think you frighten us? No. We left our villages to visit our friends on the other side of the great lake. Nothing will be able to deter us—except death!" Upon entering the harbor at Le Havre, the Osages came out on deck and thanked God for having granted them a safe crossing.

Their language is expressive, formed with guttural and aspirated sounds, resembling no other idiom.[43] Their interpreter[44]—born of a French man and an Osage woman—for whom they appear to have quite sincere affection is the only person capable of putting them in communication with the kingdom they propose to visit.

These Indians arrived in Le Havre at noon on July 27th. When they were on deck of the ship during that very hot day, a large part of the population of the city jammed onto the wharf, outer harbor, and even the spars of ships. At first this crowd troubled the savages, unaccustomed to causing such lively curiosity, but reassured by their guide they put on a good face. Since the throng was growing by the minute, a squad of military men was obliged to protect their debarkation. The entourage went to the Holland Hotel, followed by a multitude, drawn by the unusual sight, that was continually pushed back by soldiers guarding our travelers.

Once arrived at the hotel, they asked for refreshments and were served various kinds of wine, preferring the sweet wines, especially Malaga. One of them, the big soldier, although innately sober, was indisposed by this mixture. Several people were then let into the room where the Osages were resting; the Indians shook hands with them while bowing in order to give thanks for the honor they were receiving. The chief sent for the manager of the hotel in order to greet him as is their custom.

In the afternoon the Osages were taken to the country estate of

---

43. The Osage language is, in fact, related to the others in the Siouan linguistic family.

44. Paul Loise. Note this comment about "sincere affection."

the Mayor of Le Havre and there walked about the gardens, looking indifferently at the beautiful trees and rare plants embellishing
the grounds until, around the turn of one path, having recognized
a Missouri pine tree and a Louisiana poplar, their joy was great and
their expressive eyes shown with a most lively light. They then were
taken into the gallery of paintings where nothing caught their attention except a small, white-marble statue they touched several times
in order to assure themselves it was made of stone.

The next morning they visited the superb docks, and contemplated
with admiration the numerous ships floating on the water; there,
a three-masted whaling ship setting sail was pointed out to them.
"Ah!" said the youngest woman remembering they had seen an enormous whale on the ocean. "If they find the big fish that scared us,
they will be very happy!"

The same day, at 6:45 P.M., our Indians went to the theater. This
event attracted so many spectators that most of them could not find
a seat in the auditorium. Reserved for the Osages were two boxes in
the first balcony where they sat down in their natural clothes—that is
to say, the men naked to the waist, with only the two women dressed
in the fashion of their country. The spectacle began with the opera
Blaise and Babet[45] which did not seem to amuse the Indians any more
than it did the French, although it is true savages conceal their emotions with great skill, never revealing any exterior signs of boredom.
Doubtless weary of being stared at and half smothered in their boxes
in almost twenty-five degree [centigrade] heat,[46] they tried, once the
opera was over, to breathe somewhat more freely in the hall; but surrounded again, pushed, touched, and almost asphyxiated, they sought
refuge in the vestibule where they were nearly crushed against the

---

45. A comic opera by Jacques-Marie Boutet de Monvel. One of the key means
of entertaining the Indian visitors was to take them to the theater to see and
hear dramas delivered in a language they could not understand. The motivation
for such "entertainments" was likely a convenient opportunity to put the Osages
on display, for which we assume Delaunay collected a dividend.

46. Seventy-seven degrees Fahrenheit.

railings. Forced to think about retreating without waiting for the second presentation—*The Beneficiary*, played by Potier[47]—they escaped to the Place de la Comédie.[48] It was then the chief expressed his displeasure to his guides. "In my country," he said, "four soldiers suffice to keep eight or ten thousand Indians back a great distance. We will not go to any more shows[49] from now on. If we braved the dangers of the ocean, it was not in order to be smothered on the other side of the great lake."

Our overseas guests, presented to local authorities, are quite satisfied with the reception they have found. They have attended military reviews and drills at the equestrian school, and their stay in our city[50] has not yet come close to exhausting interest in them.

The End

---

47. *Le Bénéficiaire* is another minor comedy, but the actor Charles Gabriel Potier (1774–1838) was one of the best-known comic thespians of the early nineteenth century. In 1832, he appeared in a London production of the play.

48. It was standard practice to name open spaces in front of major edifices after the function of the building. Thus this theater—Comédie—stood in a square the Osages escaped to for cooler air.

49. Over the next several weeks, the Osages were taken to more stage performances, a convenient place to put them on exhibit and charge to view them. Among the plays was *Paul et Virginie*, an opera based on a popular 1787 novel by Bernadin de Saint-Pierre about two young people, living uncorrupted and isolated amidst bountiful nature, who are sent to France for education but are warped into falseness and artificiality. (One can guess just how much of this Noble Savage theme might have been conveyed to the Osages in words they did not understand.) Other productions were the comedies *Aristippi, ou Les Filets de Vulcain* and *Losiska*, an opera by Luigi Carlo Cherubini. There was also a French version of Karl von Weber's opera *Der Freishutz* titled *Robin des Bois*. More pertinent to the Osages could have been a drama called *Les Natchez*, apparently drawn from François René de Chateaubriand's 1826 book of that name and his 1801 novelette *Atala*, which tells of two "noble" Natchez Indians in Louisiana who fall in love but find their idyllic life ruptured by strictures of Christianity.

50. The personal pronoun may give a clue to challenge David Delaunay as the author of the pamphlet.

HISTORY

OF THE TRIBE

OF THE OSAGES,

SAVAGE PEOPLE OF NORTH AMERICA,

IN THE STATE OF MISSOURI

ONE OF THE UNITED STATES OF AMERICA;

WRITTEN ACCORDING TO THE SIX OSAGES IN PARIS

BY M.P.V.

Followed by the Account of the Journey of these Savages,

and by a Historical Notice on each of these Indians famous

in their tribe by their warrior exploits.

PARIS

AT CHARLES BÉCHET, BOOKSELLER,

QUAI DES AUSTINS, NO. 57

AND AT MERCHANTS OF NEW ITEMS.

IN RENNES, AT DUCHESNE, BOOKSELLER, RUE ROYALE.

1827

About the Text of

History of the Tribe of the Osages

WHOEVER MONSIEUR PAUL VISSIER (M.P.V.) was, he left few facts about himself. Because his booklet of almost fifteen thousand words was published in Paris, and because he seems to refer to Le Havre as a distant city and scarcely mentions the Osages' subsequent visit to Rouen, he was likely a resident of Paris or its environs. However, the title page of his *History of the Tribe of the Osages* indicates it was sold also in Rennes, a city a couple hundred miles west of Paris, so he instead may have been associated with that community. We do know his booklet was published sometime after August 21, 1827 (when the Osages were at the royal palace in St. Cloud, an event Vissier includes in his chapter 17), but before September 5 of the same year, when it was listed in the *Bibliographie de la France*.

Although Vissier's occasional mythological allusions suggest he was literate and educated in the classics, his capacity to compose effective—and, at times, readily comprehensible—sentences appears to have been limited. To judge from his expression, if he were a journalist or a writer of some other sort, he must have been little more than a hack. That said, his sometimes haphazard constructions may reflect only the speed with which he brought out the *History*, reprinted, based on our research, for the first time here. Whatever his occupation, he seems to have been motivated—perhaps partly by the contemporary fascination with the Noble Savage concept—to help foster a more enlightened understanding of the indigenous peoples of North America, those who were then widely called "savages," even by Vissier himself. In several places, he also manifests a progressive view—almost one of advocacy—of women, at least women in a

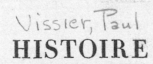

Vissier, Paul

HISTOIRE

DE LA TRIBU

DES OSAGES,

PEUPLADE SAUVAGE DE L'AMÉRIQUE SEPTENTRIONALE,
DANS L'ÉTAT DU MISSOURI,
L'UN DES ÉTATS-UNIS D'AMÉRIQUE;

ÉCRITE D'APRÈS LES SIX OSAGES ACTUELLEMENT A PARIS;

PAR M. P. V.

Suivie de la Relation du Voyage de ces Sauvages, et d'une Notice
historique sur chacun de ces Indiens célèbres dans leur tribu par
leurs exploits guerriers.

PARIS,

CHEZ CHARLES BÉCHET, LIBRAIRE,

QUAI DES AUGUSTINS, N° 57,

ET CHEZ LES MARCHANDS DE NOUVEAUTÉS.

A RENNES, CHEZ DUCHESNE, LIBRAIRE, RUE ROYALE.

1827.

Title page of *History of the Tribe of the Osages*. Author's collection.

Native culture and living an arduous life. All of this does not negate the possibility Vissier wanted to turn a quick profit from what anyone then could see was the hottest show in town.

We find no indication that his knowledge of Osage life drew upon anything other than locally and recently printed sources, and we can't be sure he even so much as caught a glimpse of the visiting Osages, since all his comments about them during their first weeks in France seem to have been taken from other published accounts. One possible exception is his remark on the modest height of the six Osages, a detail we have found nowhere else. Strange it is then, for a writer to take up a subject in a ninety-two-page work while making no apparent effort to meet even one of the people he is writing about, or any of their three tour leaders. Despite Vissier's dismissive and occasionally sarcastic tone toward the author of *Six Red Indians*, his *History*, coming sometime soon after, follows the same general outline or progression of material used by the predecessor he disparages—although at something more than twice the length. If Vissier knew who wrote *Six Red Indians*, his attitude toward the author may be evidence that it was not David Delaunay, since Vissier treats him respectfully, as in chapter 17.

Using the second edition of *Six Red Indians*, Vissier's book is largely a summary comprised of material from other sources, most of which he documents: primarily Nicolas Perrin's review in *Journal des Voyages* and Conrad Malte-Brun's commentary in his *Géographie universelle*. For a historian of his time, Vissier is unusually careful to document these sources. In his frequent idealization of Osage ways, it is clear he thought along the lines of Rousseau rather than of Count Buffon. Vissier's questionable interpretations of Osage ways are often more the result of generalizations based on other North American tribes rather than errors about the Osage tribe itself in the early nineteenth century. Further, his ideas and opinions of ancient North Americans are notably advanced for his time, thinking as he did that the monumental mounds of the United States were the work of earlier Indians rather than of long-gone European or North African immigrants and that the origin of current tribal peoples might be Asia rather than the Middle East. And, of course, he also expresses sympathy for the lot of Indian women.

In Vissier's time, the word *sauvage* (from the Latin, "of the forest") did not carry the strong pejorative sense it holds in English today. His attitude toward the Osages is fully respectful, and he typically writes with almost anthropological objectivity, consistently declining to sensationalize any potentially lurid aspect of Native culture. To cite one example, when he speaks of warfare with its attendant taking of human scalps, he does so without judgment, despite the barbarism he surely would have recognized. To the contrary, his interpretations are more likely to err in the other direction, toward the Noble Savage percept, where his naiveté and romanticizing can lead him to write: "We can readily understand that communal life among women accustomed since birth to living in the same habitation and obeying the same authority is easy and peaceful, especially when they have the same advantages; submitting to the same obligations, they know the sweetness of perfect equality."

Vissier's interpretations, whatever they are, reveal the nature of the first extensive encounters between several Osage people and Europeans in Europe; for this reason, even Vissier's distortions or occasional mistakes are useful now in helping us to visualize this particular past.

He created—however loosely—the first European attempt at a long, organized history of the Osage tribe. Even with its limitations, his work should be one of the beginning points for the study of the Osages as they at last encountered European culture on its home grounds. The rarity today of his booklet suggests its success—that is to say, the number of copies in its single printing—was small and the readership limited; considering the respect he accords the six Osages, the influence of the work probably disappointed him. In our time, nearly two centuries later, the *Histoire de le Tribu des Osages* has not been a foundational block for Osage history but merely a rare item in a bookseller's catalog.

Now, in providing this first-ever English-language translation of Vissier's *Histoire*, set in the context of its precipitating pamphlet, we hope to make a more complete and accurate account of the six Osages' European visit available to readers, the tribe, and historians who may have cited Vissier in the past but had to struggle to find and read the work.

History of the Tribe of the Osages

CHAPTER ONE

The Origin of These People

WE[1] WILL NOT ATTEMPT to resolve the major question that divides learned historians on the point of knowing whether the savages of North America are or are not descendants of the ancient patriarchs, and whether the new continent did or did not people Europe. We will limit ourselves to placing here verbatim a note printed in the *Journal des Voyages*,[2] Volume 15, pp. 367–368.

William Penn, the first to do so, expressed the opinion that the Natives of America descend from the ten tribes of Israel.[3] He based

---

1. Likely the editorial "we" rather than an indication of additional authors.

2. An influential quarterly publication about contemporaneous explorations, published in Paris from 1818 to 1829, and a major source for the *Histoire*, especially Nicolas Perrin's long 1824 review of the London edition of Hunter's *Memoirs of a Captivity*, although Vissier never mentions Perrin by name. Vissier adds a footnote: "We will often have occasion to quote this excellent work full of valuable documents and especially remarkable for its exactitude."

3. William Penn, the English colonizer of Pennsylvania, was one of numerous educated people who believed the indigenous peoples of North America may have descended from one of the so-called twelve (not ten) "lost" tribes of Israel. Others who raise the question include those mentioned by Vissier, namely:
 • Elias Boudinot, American statesman and philanthropist who wrote several religious works; relevant here is his *A Star in the West* (1816).
 • Pierre François-Xavier de Charlevoix traveled to Canada and the United States in 1720–22 and described his visit in a book published in Paris in 1744. An English translation appeared in 1761 as *Journal of a Voyage to North America*, which includes his long—and inaccurate—"discourse" on the origin of Native Americans.
 • James Adair, an eighteenth-century trader among southern tribes,

his opinion on resemblance, and even on some similarities of language, tradition, customs, rituals, and government. Doctor Boudinot, of Philadelphia, added much to W. Penn's research and presented a comparative list of Hebrew words and words taken from American dialects having the same meaning. Several of the words are identical.

Civil customs and especially religious beliefs, practices, and traditions—noted by Charlevoix, Adair, Bryan-Edwards, Beattie, Bartram, and Mackenzie—give support to Boudinot's opinion, which finds in Indian tribes a "holy ark" they carried into battle like the Israelites. Mr. Howitt, who recently published his observations made during a journey in the United States in 1819, states that he himself formerly thought this opinion somewhat whimsical but that his research led him to believe, like W. Penn, Boudinot, etcetera, that Americans descend from the children of Jacob the Patriarch.

We will add to this note the opinion of Mr. David Delaunay who took under his guidance the six Osages in France. This American colo-

_____

(cont.) wrote *The History of the American Indians*, published in 1775.

• Bryan Edwards—in the original, Vissier references "Briant-Edwards"—is the author of *The History, Civil and Commercial, of the British Colonies in the West Indies*, London, 1793. This work appeared in several editions, including a French translation; the five-volume London edition of 1819 is the most complete. The sources named in these two quoted paragraphs come originally from Emanuel Howitt's *Selections from Letters* (see below), which discusses connections between American Indian languages and culture and those of the ancient Hebrews.

• Charles Beatty published in 1768 his *Journal of a Two-Month's Tour*, describing his travels in the eastern United States.

• Botanist John Bartram's *Observations on the Inhabitants . . . and Other Matters Worthy of Notice . . . in His Travels* appeared in 1751. His son, William, published in 1791 his *Travels through . . . Carolina . . . Georgia [and] Florida*. A French translation of William's account appeared in 1799.

• Alexander Mackenzie was the second European—after Alvar Núñez Cabeza de Vaca—to travel overland from the Atlantic to the Pacific and in 1800 published his trip in *Voyages from Montreal . . . through the Continent of North America*.

• Emanuel Howitt's *Selections of Letters Written during a Tour through the United States*, London, 1820.

nel, originally from France, has been living in Louisiana [Territory] for more than twenty-seven years and has been able to observe the customs of tribes in North America.

Filled with an idea of peoples of antiquity, this officer affirms that when he arrived in America and saw the savages on the shores of the Missouri, he thought he had been carried back into the obscure centuries of ancient history.

Their simple yet rigid customs, their proud attitude, their noble air, their hospitable heart, and their way of clothing themselves brought to him, one by one, the imposing image of a Hebrew, a Greek, and an ancient Roman. In studying the customs of this people, their way of making war, the concision and eloquence of their speeches, and their auguries and worship, he found the means of perpetuating the illusion and convinced himself that, in fact, he was living with the children of Israel.

But from this idea of history, which today seems accepted, can we draw the conclusion that what we call the "Old Continent" owes its population to the "New Continent"? Once again, we will not take up this important question, the discussion of which would lead us too far from the outline we have drawn. All that we can say on this subject so important to history, is that everything concurs to prove that what we have agreed to call the "New Continent" was inhabited by a warrior people, knowledgeable of the art of fortifications and retrenchments, by a numerous population understanding the liberal arts in the highest degree and consequently enjoying the delights of civilization. Added to the number of historical testimonies attesting to these facts with certainty are the ancient monuments that overspread the shores of the Missouri; these clusters of burial pyramids[4] have been left by ancient generations to posterity as forceful proof of their passage in that part of the world.

---

4. Vissier probably refers to the four-sided, flat-topped, earthen platform mounds of the Mississippian culture (c. A.D. 700–1500), the largest of which is Monk's Mound at Cahokia in Illinois, six miles east of downtown St. Louis. Only some of these mounds were initially built for burials. Vissier's reference in his chapter 14 to "stone pyramids" is also erroneous: none of the mounds is a pyramid and none is of stone.

CHAPTER TWO

Territory

The Osage tribe is one of those living along the banks of the Missouri, a large river beginning in the Rocky Mountains near the edges of North America; after a course of twelve or thirteen hundred leagues (according to Vosgien)[5] as it waters Louisiana [Territory], it flows into the Mississippi, in Illinois, very near the city of Saint Louis. This vast country, as rich with historical memories as it is fertile with natural products and full of game, may be seen as a classic field in the art of fortifications when we consider the remains of antiquity covering it, and about which we read with great interest in the *Journal des Voyages*, Volume 6, pp. 271–294.

These historical monuments attest to a warrior people, numerous and enlightened, who cultivated the soil of Louisiana long before the discovery of this part of the world by modern nations. Who are these peoples? Could it have been a colony of Gauls or Danes who, by chance, landed in this region around the twelfth century, as certain writers think? We cannot accept this version, opposed by the knowledgeable Robertson[6] and the editors of the *Journal des Voyages*. We believe, with Mr. DeWitt Clinton,[7] president of the Literary and Philosophical Society of New York, that the remains of the ancient works covering the shores of the Missouri are sufficient proof that before the arrival of Europeans, this country held many people who lived in cities defended by fortifications, who practiced agriculture, and who were civilized to a higher degree than the savages one finds there today.

---

5. François-Baptiste Ladvocat in 1747 published under the name L'Abbé Vosgien a *Dictionnaire Géographique*, which became a standard reference source in France and was referred to simply as "Vosgien."

6. William Robertson is the author of the ten-volume *The History of America*; a complete edition appeared between 1800 and 1801.

7. See Clinton's 1818 *A Memoir on the Antiquities of the Western Parts of the State of New York*.

Lacking full knowledge of the history of this totally unknown people, the French and Dutch writers who have remarked upon the New World considered it with regard to its riches and have given us some idea of its mines and progress made by Christianity, but have told us nothing of its earlier history. In this situation we can only hazard conjectures on this interesting historical question. All that we can say with conviction is that it is impossible to believe that the 871 people who set sail in 1170 in ten ships under the command of Prince Modoc[8] extended their empire from the Copper River to the Mississippi and then were eclipsed without leaving any trace of their existence other than trenches in the ground.

Does it not in fact seem ridiculous to attribute to this little colony of Welshmen, who left for the West some six or seven hundred years ago, extensive works that cover such a great expanse from the mouth of the Mississippi to the far north? How, in such a short time, could this small group have multiplied so rapidly in spite of wars that it must have had to wage against the Natives? How, after the conquest of this immense territory, did the group cover it with cities and monuments? How could the group have caused the arts and sciences to flourish there? And especially, how could it have finally vanished without leaving traces of its blood, its art, and its civilization?

More natural is the idea that the savage peoples who live on the shores of the Missouri are descendants of an ancient people! We have already said it: The language, customs, and dress of these peoples make this version easy to accept. Let's add also that the architecture of the numerous funereal pyramids covering their country are almost unimpeachable witnesses to this historical truth.

---

8. The legend of Madoc—the more common spelling of the name—is ancient and long lasting despite no evidence—historical or archaeological—having yet been found for Welsh colonists making settlement anywhere within North America three centuries before Columbus. See Gwyn A. Williams's *Madoc: The Making of a Myth*. There are several Copper rivers to which Vissier could be referring.

CHAPTER THREE

Nations That Live along the Missouri

The tribal peoples living along the banks of the Missouri are many because each group is rather small. According to an 1820 census, reported in the *Journal des Voyages*, Volume 17, p. 123, Missouri was comprised of 66,586 people in a territory of 445,334 square miles or 148,444.66 square leagues in extent, indicating one person for every eleven square miles or 3⅔ square leagues. By assuming an equal division of territory among the inhabitants, each would have 3⅔ square leagues of land. Consequently, one can perceive that in order to occupy such a large territory, groups have to be widely separated; this remoteness must be in proportion to the population of the nations, and in the inverse proportion to their multiplicity.

The red tribes of the Missouri number thirteen, to wit: Osages, Kanzas, Sioux, Pawnee-Loups, Pawnee-Republicans, Grand-Pawnees, Poncas, Comanches, Aricaras, Mandans, Crows, Hidatsas, and Blackfeet.

Whatever connections exist between these peoples in language, dress, lifestyle, making war, hunting, form of government, and religious beliefs, they nonetheless all have individual distinguishing characteristics, which the author of the historical sketch printed in Le Havre with the title *About the Osage Indians*[9] was not careful to observe, causing him to make errors that distort the character of the tribe, whose history he attempted to write. Misled by the works of travelers he read, this author did not take into account that most of those who visited the peoples of North America—speaking in general terms about savages, without considering individual tribes—gave to [all] the savages of America the general character, traditions, and practices of whichever tribe they visited.

For example, we would get a false idea of the character of the

---

9. Vissier's "Des Indiens Osages" is a misquotation of the half title page of *Six Indiens Rouges*, where it appears as "Les Indiens Osages." His criticism of drawing particulars from generalities is apt, although he also at times assumes Osage practices from other tribes.

Osages if we judged them by the heart-rending account of the tortures suffered by Mrs. Lewis from May 25, 1815, to May 1817, an account she wrote herself, published in the United States in 1818.[10] The assassination of her husband, scalped[11] and burned before her eyes; the painful journey she made among those savages, [she] naked with her three children, the eldest of whom was barely sixteen, and the youngest whom she was still nursing; the separation of her children among the savages while she herself, having become the booty of a family of savages, was put under the domination of an old woman who took pleasure in increasing her sorrow by constantly reminding her they were going to sacrifice her children—objects of her concern and despair—and that they would soon scalp them and force her to drink from their skulls; the tortures to which they subjected her body, forcing her to walk naked through the thickest bushes and to dance on thorns and sharp stones in order to make her learn, so they said, the dance she would perform the next day at the festival celebrating the murder of her children; and a thousand other even more atrocious cruelties invented by these cannibals, which the pen refuses to outline.

Acts of this nature, revealing the cruelty of certain beings—which one can only consider as deplorable mistakes of nature—will never serve as definitive rules to characterize a nation, no matter which nation it may be.

Moreover, nothing, we quickly point out—nothing in the account of the unfortunate widow Lewis—indicates that those tyrants belonged to the Osage tribe. In the entire story of her sufferings—as recounted in the *Journal des Voyages*, Volume 2, pp. 84–103—the word "Osages" is not mentioned a single time. One thing is certain: Of all the savage tribes of North America, the Osage tribe is the closest

---

10. Published in Boston in 1817, *Narrative of the Captivity and Sufferings of Mrs. Hannah Lewis, and Her Three Children* was one of many such lurid tales quite popular in the eighteenth and early nineteenth centuries. Her account, as with many of the other captivity narratives, is of dubious authenticity and may be fictional. The tribes she mentions were not Osages but Sacs and Foxes.

11. To the term "scalped," Vissier appends a footnote: "Thus is named the operation by which the Savages of North America remove the cranium or the scalp of their victims or enemies who die in battle."

to civilization, and endowed with a humane and hospitable natural-ness,[12] so the noble members of this tribe would be, even more than we, horrified with such cold barbarity.

CHAPTER FOUR

About the Osage Tribe

This tribe, one of the nearest to the city of Saint Louis, numbers from 1,800 to 2,000 warriors, which implies a population of 20,000 souls.[13] Simple as nature but of a noble, generous, and proud char-acter, this people has only elementary notions of politics, religion, arts, and commerce. But its government, limited to the authority of an hereditary chief, has some affinity with the modern invention of representative governments. Conrad Malte-Brun[14] states (*Géographie universelle*, Volume 5, p. 410) that the Osages are divided into three classes: warriors, jugglers, and cooks.[15]

---

12. The lower Missouri Valley tribes contending with the Osages did not see them in such terms. With the arrival of French traders, the Osages became even more fierce and at times pitiless in protecting their interests. However, Paul Wil-helm wrote in his *Travels in North America:* "The Osages were less cruel than the neighbors, and for this reason human sacrifices are unknown to them. In the area of his lodge an Osage rarely murders a captured enemy, but is satisfied with the scalp of his fallen opponent" (239).

13. The Osage Nation of today gives its population in 1820 as greater than 12,000 members (www.felihkatubbe.com\osagenation).

14. Conrad Malte-Brun is the author of the eight-volume *Précis de la Géogra-phie universelle*, published from 1810 to 1824, and is a key source for Vissier.

15. Vissier uses the term *jongleur,* which in Medieval French refers to minstrels or jugglers. By extension, it came to mean "charlatan"; more tolerantly and per-haps accurately, it can be translated as "shaman" or "medicine man." In English, the terms "juggler" and "jugglery" were used by several early nineteenth-century writers in their books about North American Indians, including Henry David Thoreau. Thomas Nuttall, in his *A Journal of Travels into the Arkansas Territory during the Year 1819*, writes: "The cure of diseases, though sometimes attempted with rational application, is not unfrequently sought, among the Quapaws [related to the Osages], and many other natives of the continent, in charms and jugglery" (98). See also Vissier's chapters 9 and 10.

We feel that among a people with such limited education, the right of legitimate succession is respected only to the extent it does not encounter any illustriously ambitious man who may have enough support to overthrow the reigning dynasty, even though such revolutions rarely happen. Their form of governing, in which we can find several similarities to our modern governments and to an oligarchy, is a limited monarchy in which all affairs of importance are submitted to the assembly of warriors; this, anyway, is the opinion of Malte-Brun.

The monarch is not the only chief. Although a chief's authority extends to only a small group (because a particular tribe is not [necessarily] located in the place where the government resides but rather is divided into three villages), there is another principal chief who is the lieutenant, or if you will, the prefect of the sovereign who himself has three other chiefs under his orders. Leaders are, for the most part, distinguished warriors who owe their power to their valor as much as to their birth. These are the elements of government of the Osage tribe, under which the subjects enjoy unlimited freedom.

CHAPTER FIVE

Laws

One understands that among a people in a state of nature, law is reduced to the natural right of defense. The right of property exists among the Osages only by possession. This right is limited to avenging by force any harm caused. Since almost all the people lack an idea of the art of writing, they can have only laws prescribed by equity, with decisions delivered by weapons in hand. In this case we can say with certainty that the cause of the strongest is always the

---

(*cont.*) As for the word "cook"—*cuisinier*—Vissier took it from Malte-Brun but pointed out his notion that the role of the "cook" was more useful than that of a "juggler." Some twenty years later, Tixier employed a more pejorative term—*marmiton*, or scullery menial—to describe the same position in Osage society, even though, while cooking at ceremonies was involved, a "cook" served also as a kind of town crier, master of ceremonies, and arranger of marriages, along with a few other functions.

77

best. It would however be a grave error to conclude from this manner of delivering justice that the Osages know no other law than that of force. They do have some precise ideas about property rights, and one can even assert that they respect it more than civilized peoples in whom excess and indolence have introduced vices unknown to savage peoples. Almost never, except on members of an outside group, do the Osages take the occasion to actively repress theft of horses or game.

Having no other means of bringing outside malefactors to justice, the Osages use on them or on their tribe the natural right of reprisal, which, being carried out only by armed force, is decided in favor of the strongest. However, with regard to a fellow tribesman who commits a theft and so harms a brother—something difficult to imagine since what is not common property among them is more or less mixed up together thereby making theft more difficult—if theft is determined, the victim is authorized to punish the guilty, and the punishment is swift and dreadful.

CHAPTER SIX

Arts, Agriculture, Commerce

It is not in the liberal arts, which are quite unknown in the Missouri country, that one must seek proof of genius in the nation that concerns us. The mechanical arts themselves are practiced there only for the indispensable needs of the basic preservation of life. Thus architecture—for us the highest of the arts—is reduced among the North American [Indians] to the skill of driving some pointed posts in the ground and covering them with branches and tree bark in order to protect the domicile from wild beasts and intemperate weather. Such lodgings they call "wigwams."

A mat of reeds or the skin of a bison or bear makes a bed on which the Osage and his family give themselves restful sleep without worry. The rest of the furnishings correspond to the simplicity of a bed; a copper pot and a few clay dishes make up the belongings of the North American Savage.

To these objects, however, one must add their arms and agricultural implements. The latter objects are limited to a few picks and hatchets supplied by American merchants in exchange for pelts; some tools serve to turn the earth, others to clear woods and to cut timber. Women, who do all the domestic work, during certain seasons also sow corn and pumpkins, which, according to Malte-Brun, are the only vegetables in their diet, and if they eat some other kinds, those are not cultivated but produced spontaneously in the earth.

Arms, about which we will talk under the heading of warriors, are also fundamentally simple—at least those crafted by savages. Their clothes are things they excel in making. However, if one allows an exception for the whimsical taste in their choice of materials, their industry in this regard is limited to the art of sewing, a talent of these women who are the only ones to practice it and who are far less skilled than our experienced seamstresses.

Men shave their heads with the exception of a strip of hair they leave growing on the top to which they attach a feather and a cylinder of silver or tin; they wear a headband of woodpecker beaks or duck bills painted blue-green and red. They paint their faces with four colors: red, blue-green, white, and black. Their dress consists of a wool blanket draped over the shoulders in the manner of the ancient Romans; they cover their legs with large leather leggings fastened to a belt to which is also attached a strip of red cloth that hangs between their legs. Footwear is made from tanned deer or bison skin. The remainder of men's ornaments is composed of bands worn on their arms, a necklace formed by several cords strung with small beads of shell or glass, and one or more round or crescent medallions dangling to the stomach, sometimes as far as the navel.

Women do not cut their hair at all, instead keeping it long, flat, and hanging down, divided on top of the head by a part painted red with vermilion. They, like the men, wear necklaces, ear pendants, medallions on the breast bone, and arm bands. Their tunics reach from the neck to the knees. When women cannot obtain material to make a tunic, they cover their breasts with a piece of calico, chintz, or sheeting, and, like men, wear a loin cloth to cover themselves from the hips to the back of the knees. They also have mitas[16]

---

16. It is unclear to what language, if any, this term belongs.

of buffalo or bison skin. When they are able to obtain scarlet cloth in order to make themselves a kind of pantaloon they decorate with brightly colored ribbons and sew with special stitches, they are much delighted. This finery, coarsely produced, does not indicate a highly developed industry, especially when we realize that all the cloth and tools necessary to make clothing are procured by the Osages through trade with white men.

Among the Osages, commerce is no more an art than is agriculture, limited as it is to trading products of their hunts for objects of little cost. Totally surrendering to the cupidity of the white men with whom they trade, the goods the Osages do furnish are highly sought after by speculators. In return for objects of small cost, the Indians supply furs of great value, the only things they can offer for exchange.

Commerce, which they call "trade," is accomplished in their land through fur dealers who go into their villages to tender arms and ammunition, ordinary and brightly colored cloth, wool blankets, and hardware. Sometimes the Indians go to either St. Louis or New Orleans to sell their furs; when they make these trips, they travel down the Missouri on rafts carrying their merchandise.

In commercial transactions, they manifest a loyalty we can regret not to find in civilized man. Although their bartering is always transacted on the spot, sometimes it happens that savages who go to St. Louis and New Orleans are tempted by various objects they see in houses, which they enter brashly and without invitation. The resident is eager to offer some object because ordinarily the Indians desire things of little value. The grateful savage, feeling obligated to the giver, never fails to bring him the product of the next hunt and thus pays a hundred times more than the worth of the object received.

We have said that the Osage people are comprised of three classes: warriors, jugglers, and cooks. Now let us discuss what constitutes warriors, jugglers, and cooks.

CHAPTER SEVEN

Warriors

Especially among savage peoples, the maxim "every man is a soldier" has an accurate application. Perpetually required to have arms to repel aggression and to defend liberty, life, and possessions, savages live in a state of continual war. Among them, bravery is the highest virtue and the use of weapons, the highest art; bodily strength, dexterity, agility, and toughness are the primary physical qualities. He who has all these capacities is the most respected man because he is the most feared. All efforts of education are designed to instill these advantages, the only strengths truly useful to natural man.

Boys under the age of nine or ten do nothing, since their first years are consecrated to the development of bodily strength. From the age of ten to twelve, they are assigned the task of caring for the horses, leading them to pasture and guarding them. This work, by having them do exercise favorable to good health, also has the advantage of making them familiar with the animal that will soon become the companion of their work as warriors and the source of their wealth.

When they attain their thirteenth birthday, they practice handling the bow and arrow, which they skillfully use on rabbits, squirrels, and birds. At fifteen, they go hunting and into battle with their fathers to become familiar with the sight of carnage, although they do not [actually] take part until age eighteen because only then are they strong enough to repel the vigorous attack of the enemy and deliver decisive blows. Besides these sure means of shaping a boy to the business of arms, savages also take effective care to deflect from him all that could unnerve his spirit and weaken his body.

The highest condition a woman requires of a suitor seeking to please her—that of prowess in war—makes love itself a powerful vehicle in forming a warrior. Among the Osages, a young man without any claims to glory who would offer his love would be disdainfully rebuffed by the woman and her family, and he would become an object of derision for the whole village. But if he presents himself with a scalp in hand, he is sure of pleasing and will soon be made happy.

Among civilized peoples, dancing is a powerful means of seduction leading directly to permissiveness. Among the Osages, however, it is another way of maintaining their robust vigor and exalting their warrior spirit. What they consider dancing is not limited to whirling in the arms of a woman and sensually going around a room (an action in which art is joined to nature, thereby provoking a breakdown of morals), nor is dancing limited to jumping up and down in front of a woman while making more or less ridiculous contortions of the body or some fancy movements. Among the savages of North America, dance has a graver character and a more useful purpose. Intended to represent an action, dancing is dramatic in its several forms. The hunting dance, representing deeds of the hunter in different perilous situations joined to gestures, shows the events along with an account of the hunter's anguish and perils, and the results of his efforts.

The war dance is the most impressive of all, or perhaps the most terrifying.[17] It involves fencing, and, in this respect, one can associate it with a match between our weapons masters. The dancers appear fully armed and have a sham battle. This also partakes of drama because the participants often interrupt themselves in order to recount and depict the action of their gloriously waged exploits in combat. These practical amusements, which all young men are eager to attend, maintain in them the love of glory and increase their impatience to show valor.

It is also with a war-like purpose that they paint their faces, pluck out their beards and eyebrows, and shave their heads. Among the savages, for whom courage alone rather than physical strength characterizes the warrior, all facial hair—symbol of animal might—is carefully removed. The head itself is shaved, leaving a tuft of hair shaped like the comb of a Greek helmet on top of the head (because of religious respect for the right of the victor to scalp the vanquished) as a way of facilitating the removal of this trophy.

So it is that everything among this people comes together to shape the warrior. Without being any the less filled with the innate senti-

---

17. For a detailed description of an Osage war dance, see Charles William Janson's *Stranger in America*, 1933 edition, 231–32.

ment of self-preservation than is civilized man, the North American savage is proud to die on the field of honor. He who falls gloriously under enemy blows is assured of leaving a revered memory and of enjoying a future as a noble man.

The Osage male thus fashioned for war is always ready to wage it. The slightest cause is enough to give him a legitimate reason to flex his muscles. These men, provided with a fertile territory and abundant game, never point to a quarrel about boundaries as a cause of war, nor do they ever take up arms for a political principle or some religious notion. In this regard, they are more reasonable than refined civilized peoples. But the incursion of an outsider—followed by theft, kidnapping, or murder by a member of a neighboring tribe—or hunting on the grounds of the Osages are frequent reasons for going off to fight.

Here is the way they take up arms: He who laments the violent death of one of his family leaves the village and builds a small lodge somewhat apart and there gives himself up to grief; after this period of sorrow, he thinks of vengeance. To second his project he chooses from his tribe the brother he judges to be the most worthy by manifestation of warrior qualities. He then sends for him and says, "You see my sorrow. The Sioux (or another people) slaughtered my father. Since then I have had no rest. His shadow cries to me to avenge him, and I want to go to war against the assassins of my father. Certain of your valor, I have chosen you to be the leader of this enterprise. You will not refuse me." This choice, being a great honor, is always accepted, and the one designated by the partisan (as they call the one who summons the warriors) becomes the general for the campaign.

This general, known as the "chief of the party," in turn summons about twenty braves and explains to them the partisan's plan, sets a day for beginning, and gives them the task of informing the warriors of the tribe. The day before departure, the warriors, some three or four hundred, come to the lodge of the partisan to drop off their leggings and shoes (mitas and moccasins); the next morning at daybreak the warriors hurry in from all sides to the partisan's lodge, the usual place of rendezvous for the departure. When all warriors are gathered together, they set out for the village of the malefactor. The partisan goes unarmed, carrying on his back and suspended from his neck, the skin of a stuffed sparrow-hawk covered with a tanned, white deer hide. All this is wrapped with matting.

As soon as the party discovers either the enemy on patrol or the village they propose to attack, the warriors stop and rest. Then the partisan approaches the chief of his followers and gives him the bird wrapped in the tanned skin, but he keeps the matting and puts it on his back. The bird is the augur that foresees the outcome of the battle. Here is the way it is consulted: The chief of the war party lies down on his back and places the bird on his chest, its beak pointed towards his mouth; he then sleeps in this position. As soon as he awakens, now surrounded by the warriors, the partisan approaches him and questions him about the revelations the augur made during his sleep. The chief replies; almost always the predictions are favorable.

When it is time for combat, the chief of the war party calls together the warriors and all listen with eager attention. He summons the one he most esteems and covers him with the deer skin used to envelop the augur, which the honored man now keeps and carries on his back. To him who carries the hide, he says: "I have chosen you among all our brothers to be second in command because I have more confidence in you than in any other. You will be in command on my left."

Then speaking to the partisan to whom he gives a musket, powder, and lead (carried until then by a young man), he says: "We are going forth to avenge you. You will be in command on my right." The partisan replies: "I gave you the task of directing the war because I judged you to be the most capable of leading us to victory and the most worthy of leading us. It is to you I entrusted the bird, seer of the future. It predicted for you a brilliant success. You told us of these happy revelations. Each of us will do his duty." Then speaking to the warriors: "And you, my brothers, for me you have left your lodges and hasten into battle to avenge the death of my father. You have seen my tears; you have had pity for me. The Master of Life will augment your courage. He foresees victory for us. He never deceives. Trust Him as you trust my gratitude to you." Then, after a short prayer to the Master of Life, they go into combat in three squads deployed in a front along the same line. At the center of each squad, and in advance, is the respective leader. The middle column is commanded by the chief of the war party, the left wing by the lieutenant of his choice (the bearer of the deer skin), and the right wing by the partisan. These three chiefs, pouring down on the enemy or on the village, exhort the warriors they lead to advance and never flee.

When they confront the enemy on the open plain and in battle, combat is deadly, as each warrior burns with the desire to take scalps or kick an enemy who has bitten the dust. The action of being the first to touch an enemy[18] fallen on the field of battle is a feat of prowess the Osages honor; it is—after the honor of killing, which alone gives the right of scalping—part of taking a prisoner, an action they revere, for it proves that one was in a place of danger and ready to sacrifice his life for the victor.

Prisoners are treated with the utmost humanity. Led to the conqueror's village, they are given to families who have lost relatives. There, carefully watched at first in order to prevent them from escaping, they soon become an object of affection to the family that adopts them before they are finally assimilated with all the other residents. There is, however, an exception to this generous conduct: when those who have taken prisoners are pursued, and guarding the captives would remove useful warriors from combat, those prisoners are sacrificed to mutual defense by being immediately put to death.

When ready to do battle in the village, a warrior surprises the enemy with sharp cries and shouts rather than meeting him on the plain. Vengeance is limited to the killing of fifteen or twenty people, after which the warriors withdraw, taking prisoners and spoils of war. But if the attack fails and the assailants are driven away, leaving warriors behind as prisoners, women in the besieged village react as described in the pamphlet from Le Havre on page 6 [p. 45]: "One can hardly conceive that females who have such a mild appearance, can be so frightening and so cruel when they fall upon an enemy prisoner."

Women, we point out, never join a war party and consequently can never—outside this situation—*fall upon* a prisoner. Impassioned by the horror of the carnage they witness and by picturing perils to which their husbands, brothers, and children were exposed, women

---

18. This action is well known as "counting coup" and earned a warrior distinction.

in their fury can only sometimes massacre prisoners, but they never give in to any act of cruelty in cold blood. On the contrary, as attested to by all travelers, most often women who lament the loss of a relative killed in combat, adopt a prisoner and bestow on him all the affection they once had for the person they lost.

But there must be exceptions to this conduct so noble and so humane. Because the fate of the captive is left to the family that lost one of its members, it sometimes happens in the first flush of sorrow that the family agrees to sacrifice a prisoner to the spirit of the dead relative, as is told in the almost unique example from the account of the widow [Hanna] Lewis. Still, these acts of deplorable vengeance are so rare, one can consider them as exceptions to the general rule we just stated.

CHAPTER EIGHT

About Hunters

Hunting, one of the principal means of both wealth and subsistence for the Osages, with its perils and fatigues, is yet another occupation of young males who are active, vigorous, and skillful in the art of handling weapons. That is to say, it is the work of the warrior class. Charged with defending the Native land, they also must provide for the needs of the families.

Trained in this art from childhood, young men are adroit and resolutely courageous. Their weapons for hunting are the bow and the musket. They deliver an arrow with such force, it often pierces the body of even the largest animal and falls to earth some distance away on the side opposite the hunter, a fact attested to by travelers who have witnessed it.

Abundant game consists of bison (wild cattle), which gather in herds sometimes reaching fifty or sixty animals, buffalo, bears, beavers, and so forth. Horses are also hunted, but the savages seek to take them alive to be broken and trained for use in hunting. To master this proud animal, they try to surprise it by approaching near enough to throw a rope with a slip knot around its neck. This hunt is done on foot, the Osages being great walkers, covering thirty to forty-five leagues a day. They walk quickly, guiding themselves only by the sun and the stars, going straight to their destination, without avoiding obstructions in their way, whether broken terrain or dense forests. When they have finished hunting, often far from their habitations, they pause to orient themselves, never making a mistake in their calculations. As soon as they know what route they must take, they travel on a straight line to reach their destination. Hunting ordinarily requires several days, sometimes even months.

In groups of fifteen, twenty, or even fifty or sixty, they usually hunt on foot, except when pursuing bison, which they do on horseback. Once they discover a herd of these animals, they stop to make plans and to address a short prayer to Houackanda,[19] the Master of Life, in order to ask him to support their efforts. Riding steeds perfectly trained to surround the herd, they shoot arrows so well, they almost always hit the mark. They aim for the shoulder of the bison. When the wounded animal becomes furious, twists in all directions, and tries to charge the hunter, he guides his horse in the same direction, executing all the movements of the bison, while continuing to shoot arrows until he has put the animal down; then he leaves it to pursue another.

Based on the account of one traveler, the author of the Le Havre pamphlet exclaims on page 6 [p. 45]: Does the Indian go hunting? . . . He almost always returns without bringing back his prey. His wife takes off his leggings and shoes; she washes his feet, fills his pipe, and awaits his orders. My kill is at such and such a distance, the savage tells her (the author should have added "and in such and such a direction"). The woman soon sets out, and what is singular, is that, in these immense empty lands, the unfortunate savage woman never goes astray; she returns carrying the game.

It is impossible to take this account literally: the product of the

---

19. The name is usually Wakonda or Wah'Kon-Tah, "the Great Mysterious." Paul Wilhelm wrote of the Osage tribe in his *Travels in North America:* "Excepting the Pawnees, no Indian tribe venerates the Highest Being, the Master of Life, as fervently as they, and their priests are therefore held in high esteem. Indeed no Osage undertakes an important transaction without asking the advice of the priests and without preparing himself by fasting, severe penance, and sacrifice" (239).

hunt is most often too bulky and heavy for a woman to carry or even drag. Rectifying the thoughtless assertion of the author from Le Havre, let us amend it to: "sometimes" or "rarely," rather than "almost always," when the hunter, tired after a long trip, brings down small game a short distance away, he leaves it for his wife to fetch.

CHAPTER NINE

About Jugglers

Jugglers[20] form the least numerous class. They devote themselves to medicine, receiving their diploma from the Master of Life, who, in a dream, reveals to them their calling to heal their brothers. Their art is even more guesswork than that of our doctors because it is based only on personal observations augmented perhaps by superstition. Medicines are limited to the use of a few plants.

The knowledge of shamans is not confined to the art of healing because they are also priests—or rather magicians—and interpreters of dreams. In this respect, they exercise a very great influence on social affairs. They are moreover endowed with the faculty of divination, foreseeing the future, which opens itself to their minds by means of certain sorceries. Finally, like the augurs and oracles of ancient peoples, they exploit the credulous simplicity of their compatriots, as Malte-Brun attests in his *Géographie universelle*, Volume 5, p. 410.

As medicine men, they take charge in cases of difficult childbirth, and are also called in for serious illnesses. As sorcerers, they are consulted in public affairs, and when there is a question of general war, they predict the outcome unveiled to them by the Master of Life in their dreams. As priests, they preside at the Corn Dance, a ceremony meant to attract the blessing of heaven on the seed.

---

20. See note 15.

CHAPTER TEN

About Cooks

The cooks,[21] of more use and more numerous than the jugglers, render services both positive and somewhat practical to the nation. In this respect, they are more worthy of esteem than the imposters of which we have just spoken. These men—unable to go to war or on hunting trips, and with no family to see to their needs—voluntarily dedicate themselves to the cult of Comus.[22] The profession they exercise puts them in a kind of domestic category, but in order to practice successfully, they must be appointed by an important personage, such as the sovereign, a village chief, an illustrious warrior, or an affluent man.

Their appointment to this work is made with great solemnity in the presence of all village inhabitants gathered for this occasion. He who appoints a cook gives him furs, furnishings, clothes, and a horse. The wealth of the man naming a cook is apparent in the largesse of the endowment he gives, proving that among the savages themselves, wealth has luster and creates admiration. Cooks are sometimes attached to the service of an individual, but most often they are not, instead consecrating their work to public service.

Besides the most essential art of preparing foods—which among this people is limited to cooking kernels of green corn mixed with bison fat, boiling pumpkins, roasting meat, and making soup from a species of big red ant, a dish like pudding *à la chipolata*[23]—cooks are

---

21. See note 15 and our introduction, 7–8.

22. The Roman god of feasting and nocturnal revelry.

23. *Chipolata* is a type of small pork-sausage made in imitation of ones in Italy. The term may derive from the Italian word *cipollata* to refer to a type of sausage stew seasoned with onions (*cipollini*). *Chipolatas* can still be found on French tables.

Vissier adds a footnote:

> We assume these ants to be *formica cephalotes—cephalopodus—* described by Mr. de Lamarck as a large species, often traveling in innumerable swarms, inhabiting South America and also abundant along the shores of the Osage River. To get these ants, the cooks send women

charged with organizing feasts. An invitation is made in these terms: *So and so is giving a feast; come, and enjoy his munificence.* Refusal is an offense. The cooks serve the food and are public criers to make proclamations; in another chapter we will see it is through them marriages are arranged.

We will not close here without recounting the way the Osages treat Americans who visit them from the United States. When an American goes to an Osage village, custom *requires* he go first to the lodge of the chief, who gives him an eager welcome and does the noteworthy honor of letting him smoke his pipe; then a feast is prepared, from which the Osage, like the ancient patriarchs, takes the first serving. The notables of the village, following the example of the chief, invite the outsider to other feasts; the guest sometimes receives twelve to fifteen invitations in a single day. He is obliged to go to each; otherwise he risks the danger of doing a grave injustice to Amphitryon.[24] Each invitation is proffered by the cook, who makes it in these terms: *Come and eat, so-and-so is giving a feast; come and enjoy his generosity.* (Malte-Brun, *Géographie universelle*, Volume 5, p. 412).

(*cont.*) out at daybreak when this industrious creature is ready to leave the nest to look for food; the women stick their arms into the nest as far as possible so the ants can cling to them and thus be delivered to her who brushes them off into a vessel designed to contain them.

We have found no evidence of the Osages or any other North American Indians using any type of ant for culinary purposes, although the Aztecs ate ant larvae (egg cases) as a delicacy. Chevalier de Lamarck (Jean Baptiste Pierre Antoine Monet) is the great French naturalist whose many works presented new zoological descriptions.

24. A character in Molière's comedy demonstrating the importance of dining well and inviting others to share in the bounty.

CHAPTER ELEVEN

About Women

Women, called "squaws," have an extremely laborious existence, their least pursuits being the duties of maternity and domestic care. In addition to the cultivation of crops, they accompany their husbands on hunting trips when the whole tribe goes to establish a camp; they are loaded down with the overwhelming burden of field equipment, furnishings, and household utensils. They often stagger under the weight, but their husbands are insensitive to their fatigue and do not relieve them. Having arrived at the campground, the women cannot so much as take a break from the tiring work of setting up the bivouac. Yet, even though an Osage woman has a laborious existence, she enjoys the highest respect from her husband and receives his faithful friendship, and he is always ready to avenge affronts she might receive from others. Among these women, the feelings of maternity exist in all their strength and affections—shared among their husbands and their children—feelings intense and constant. Always gentle, humane, generous, hospitable—unless offended in their tender solicitude for their children or given uneasiness for the life of their husbands—the women will turn furious when they become anxious about loved ones. This is the reason they go to extremes against enemy prisoners who have troubled the tranquility of their village through pillage and murder.

Chastity is another of their virtues; maidens calmly await the age of marriage, which, as among us, is from fifteen to twenty for women, and eighteen to twenty-five for men. A maiden acting without moral restraint before marriage will be scorned by her compatriots and abandoned by her family who will then pursue the defiler; he will become known at the moment of childbirth when the girl is obliged to reveal the father of the child. This man shares the scorn and abjection into which his partner has fallen, and he, like her, is shunned and can no longer marry, unless some shining exploits in war or numerous successful hunting trips emphatically wipe out the memory of his mistakes. This is especially true among the Osages. As for the girl, deprived of such means of regaining consideration, she is forever cast into the ranks of Messalines[25] to drag out her life in shame and have only fleeting and clandestine contact with men.

Adultery in women—a [potential] capital offense the husband immediately avenges both on his wife and her accomplice—is extremely rare in this tribe. As one can see from what is written above, the Osages have about the same principles we do concerning chastity and adultery in women.

CHAPTER TWELVE

About Children

From what we have said in the course of this work, there remains little for us to recount in this chapter devoted to the history of childhood among the Osages.

Women are assisted during childbirth by matrons, or rather by godmothers and neighbors knowledgeable from personal experience. When a birth is laborious, they send for a doctor, who is, as we said earlier, a grossly ignorant shaman who—thanks to his revelations—believes himself capable of anything. He is a sort of *omnis homo*[26] whose art—being reduced to imposture—brings no remedy other than persuasion, but at least gives confidence. He encourages resignation to suffering, raises the patient's spirit, and gives her strength to tolerate pain. Nature does the rest.

The doctor does not operate in any way during childbirth, instead limiting himself to casting spells and prescribing the application of a certain plant of practical properties, which, placed on the belly of the

---

25. Messalina, third wife of Roman emperor Claudius, was infamous for her licentiousness.

26. Everyman.

woman, facilitates delivery; it is Robert's herb (*Geranium robertia-num*)[27] for the Osages; midwives carry out the prescription.

Childbirth accomplished, the infant is entrusted to his mother, who breast-feeds him until the age of fifteen or eighteen months. Often these little fellows run after their mothers and clamor to be suckled. This extended nursing[28] is not unknown among us, where some mothers do not wean their children until the age of two; among the savages, the reason is the lack of food suitable to the delicacy of the stomach during the first months of childhood.

These unfortunate children—victims, like many of our children, under the care of their mothers—are swaddled, and (I will suggest) even packaged and bound in such a way to prevent movement of any limb, which singularly harms the development of their continuously compressed organs. Thus wrapped, they are placed on a prepared fur attached to a suspended plank surmounted by a circle from which hangs a piece of cotton print or some other cloth in order to protect them from insects and diminish the brightness of daylight too intense for their weak eyes. Their martyrdom is quite similar to that of our own children.

As soon as they are able to crawl, the infants are delivered from that torture, remaining naked. Once they can walk, they are given mitas and later clad in a dress or blouse worn until the children are old enough to go to war. At the age of six months, their ears are pierced with several closely spaced little holes that are joined when the child is seven or eight to form a single perforation that dominates the entire circumference of the ear.

At age eight or nine, the education of boys and girls is the same—that is to say, they receive none and are not given any work. But after that age, girls are placed under the direction of their mothers and turned to domestic tasks, their only occupation for the rest of life.

---

27. While there is in North America a plant today called herb Robert, we have not found any Native uses of it in parturition. There was medicinal application of a related plant, wild or spotted geranium (*Geranium maculatum*). Many tribes did employ several other unrelated herbs to assist a childbirth.

28. Because nursing can help suppress ovulation, breast feeding is sometimes used as a type of birth control throughout the world.

Everyone studiously tries to make them into good housewives and prepare them to become good mothers.

At age nine, boys are placed under the direction of fathers and begin to care for horses, leading them to graze. The boys practice using the bow and arrow by hunting rabbits, squirrels, and birds, as we have already said. This sort of sport is a useful pastime for them as they do it while watching over horses in the grassland. All the little boys from the same village keep their mounts in the same pasture,[29] and each little guardian is responsible for his family's ten to twenty horses kept in a large, communal pasturage. As long as the [tribe's] horses, numbering from 1,500 to 2,000 [animals], find enough grazing in the same locality, they are led to it, but when it's depleted, they are taken to another place on the immense prairies. At the age of sixteen, when boys stop caring for horses and go hunting with their fathers, they are armed with a musket to shoot roe deer, fallow deer,[30] bison, buffalo, and bears. From age eighteen to twenty, they go to war and get married.

CHAPTER THIRTEEN

Love and Marriage

Aside from the chapter about warriors, this one is the most interesting in the history of the Osages and offers a picture of unusual and curious ceremonies revealing the mores of the tribe.

Love is ardent but of short duration, for as soon as a young man has shown his valor in war and his skill in hunting, he thinks about becoming established. It is rare that he sighs more than four or five months over the maid he wishes to link to his lot, or if he does sigh, it is in secret, because as soon as he comes back from battle with some distinction—or if lacking occasion to prove his worth in com-

---

29. Here, in parentheses and italic type, Vissier adds the word *haussan*, which he appears to translate from an unstated language as "point" or "pasturage."

30. Roe and fallow deer are Eurasian and do not occur naturally in North America. The Osages did, of course, hunt white-tail and mule deer as well as elk.

bat has earned his reputation as a hunter—he is sure to make his love acceptable should he address a family on the same level as his own. The way he offers his hand in marriage may appear bizarre, as does the way others celebrate his marriage, although these ceremonies are filled with dignity and nobility, and owe much to the customs of ancestors. However, they are less extraordinary than the result of the marriage which confers authority to the husband over his wife's entire family and all their property.

If equality is the rule among members of the Osage tribe, it is not as absolute as we might think: numerous distinctions exist based on the importance of family and wealth, and even of birth, as we have seen in the right of succession to the throne thereby established. One can say the same about lesser dignitaries, village chiefs, and other lesser chiefs. These privileged families form a patrician caste surrounded by a certain distinction.

Marriages below one's station are rare among the Osages who are careful to conserve the reputation of their family. Thus, when a young man proposes to unite himself to a girl, he tells his oldest brother about his project, or if lacking an older brother, he tells his uncle (because the father has little authority in families, the uncle is invested with power if there is no son old enough to exercise influence). The brother or uncle makes known the object of the young man's wishes and consults his family about the choice. Whenever conventions oppose a proffered marriage, the young man must give up his wish and make another choice.

Once the young man receives his uncle's approval, he announces the marriage to the rest of his family who limit their reactions to congratulations. Then he calls in the cooks and, according to his wealth, gives them a number of horses. This can be as many as twenty—the greater the number, the more his future wife is honored. The young man instructs the cooks to lead the horses to the doorway of the woman he wants to marry and to tie them there. The cooks' mission is limited to securing the horses to the entrance of the girl's lodge and saying they come on behalf of so and so.

She understands what that means and tells her uncle or her brother, who gives his consent—if he approves of the marriage. If he refuses to consent, the horses are sent back to the domicile of the young man, who is then forced to renounce the marriage. If the request is accepted by the girl and her family, the horses are distributed among her relatives who are quick to offer the future groom presents of comparable value. These gifts consist of horses, scarlet cloth, guns, jewelry, and household utensils.

This exchange takes place by means of the cooks the day before the arranged marriage ceremony. The following day, between four and five o'clock, the relatives of the bride, after having adorned her with her best finery, lead her, mounted on one of their best horses, to the young man's lodge. She is preceded by the cooks who announce the marriage as they go along.

The mother and sisters of the groom hurry to meet and compliment her, help her dismount, and greet her with the titles of "daughter" and "sister-in-law." They ask her to come into their home, inviting her family as well, and they have her sit on a new mat—a most beautiful one—spread out in the middle of the room to receive her. There they quickly remove all her clothes and ornaments and immediately replace them with others equally fine and new. Those she wore will become property of the mother and sisters of the groom because everything remains in their lodge. The remainder of the day is spent in congratulations and family feasting. In the evening, after the feasts, the married couple goes to the nuptial bed and consummates the marriage—at least this is probable.

The next morning, around nine o'clock, the young woman must again be separated from the husband to whom she owes the joys of marriage. This will be their last separation and it will not be for long, thus strongly contributing to making it tolerable. Between nine and ten in the morning, dressed in wedding clothes given to her by the mother and sisters of her husband, the bride gets on a horse and returns to her father—[considered] no less pure than when she left the day before—although she does not carry back all that she had at her departure. She has exchanged her uncertainties preceding the marriage for wonderful memories. Her father receives her, and if his look, both affectionate and severe, does not make her blush, the fault lies with the gods who do not allow these nymphs on the banks of the Osage River to blush. However, if the consistency of the color of her face, symbol of her constant affections, prevents her from showing any signs of troubled modesty (which might bother her upon returning to the paternal lodge), this anxiety is revealed in her bright and exhausted eyes scarcely daring to meet the glance of the observant father. He might address his daughter with the provocative speech of Parny[31] to his Eleanor the morning after their marriage:

> At last, my dear Eleanor,
> You have tasted this charming pleasure
> Which you feared, even while desiring it.
> In tasting it, you were still afraid.
> Well, tell me, what is frightful about it?
> After it, what does it leave in your soul?
> A slight trouble, a tender memory,
> The surprise of a new flame,
> A sweet regret, and especially a desire.

Soon after the return of the concerned bride to the paternal roof, her relatives send a cook, natural master of all ceremonies of important days, to invite her husband to join them. He immediately obeys this invitation and goes on foot. As soon as the family sees him, the father, brother, and uncle of his wife approach; greet him with the familial names of "son-in-law," "brother-in-law" and "nephew;" and invite him to come into his new home.

Once he is inside, his father-in-law addresses him in these terms: "Your family and mine agree with each other. By your valor in war and your skill in hunting, as well as by your conduct, you pleased my daughter, and you made her proud to be known as your wife. Come live with us. All that we have belongs to you. From now on, as head of our family and owner of our belongings, all that we kill in the hunt and all the bounty of war will become your property."

The son-in-law, by entering into his wife's family, becomes the head, and each member must obey him. As the new proprietor of the entire patrimony of his wife's family, all members work for him and

---

31. Evariste de Parny became known in 1778 for his *Poésies érotiques*. In 1827 his *Oeuvres choisies* appeared posthumously; Vissier's quotation comes from the first poem in that book.

acquire only for him, and they in turn become proprietors of all that he himself acquires. The game the son-in-law kills while hunting and the booty he gains in war are divided between members of the family, who can use it however they wish, without being obliged to consult with him about satisfying their whims. With these exceptions, he is absolute master of all other things, with the obligation, however, of providing for the needs of all. One can compare his authority to that of the father of a family in France, whose wife and children must obey him and who, more than being just an administrator of communal goods, may sell the goods without consulting anyone else.

This completely pastoral institution obliges family members to give careful attention to the choice of a new master. Apart from the interest of the girl—so often sacrificed among civilized peoples to the frivolous desire to arrange a rich marriage—among the Osages, every relative is directly interested in a choice almost always justified by the qualities of the new husband. The power of the head of the family would be poorly founded if it could be shared by the husband or husbands of one or several of his wife's sisters because sharing authority could produce domestic dissension, which would soon make communal life intolerable. The Osages have prevented this unfortunate circumstance by authorizing the husband of the oldest daughter to become the husband of all the other daughters. Polygamy is permitted by the institutions of this people; not only does an Osage have the rights of a husband over all his wife's younger sisters, but he may also take as many concubines as he wants—although holding no rights over his concubines' sisters.

Having consecrated the principle that the son-in-law—a young warrior, active, and of good character—will assume paternal authority from the day of his marriage so that the family always will be governed by a vigorous man capable of earning respect for it, the Osages authorize the head of the family to take several wives [sisters of his first wife] in order to fulfill the goal of maintaining only one head of a family. This objective would be completely unattainable if the man were allowed to take wives from other households; were he to become head of several families, he might have some preference harmful to the others. Many more understandable reasons could show the defect of a practice that would make it impossible to sustain.

Thus, the husband of the oldest daughter can have several wives, but only if his wife has sisters. In this case, after two years of marriage, he becomes the legitimate spouse of the second sister. If there is a third or a fourth or more, he does not automatically become the spouse; rather he must again consult the family retaining the means of holding him within the limits of good administration. If he behaves as a despot, or if he administers poorly, in order to escape from his tyranny or his wastefulness, the family may choose another master, thereby impoverishing him; but this rarely occurs and then only when there are strong reasons for unhappiness. The husband of several women is supposed to have the same consideration for each of them and to take them by equal turns to the conjugal bed, unless sickness prevents one of them from exercising this precious right, the enjoyment of which they highly esteem.

We can readily understand that communal life among women accustomed since birth to living in the same habitation and obeying the same authority is easy and peaceful, especially when they have the same advantages; by submitting to the same obligations, they know the sweetness of perfect equality.

CHAPTER FOURTEEN

About Old Age, Sickness, and Death

Among a sober people who do not use any strong liquor and consider distilled spirits a poison and drunkenness an object of horror, a person should live a long life. This is in fact what happens in the Osage tribe. From the age of forty on, a man, exempt from the fatigues of war and its risks, goes hunting only as a means of distraction and passes the remainder of his life in pleasant activities in the midst of his family, surrounded with the esteem of his compatriots and the veneration of his children. These savages have a sacred adage: "obedience and respect to old age."

When an Osage becomes seriously ill, he becomes the object of his relatives' solicitude, and they procure for him all the resources of medicine, which unfortunately are reduced for them to charms and divinations even less effective than medicinal remedies among civilized peoples. Lacking positive cures, the family of the dying man lavishes its affections by surrounding his pallet, exhorting him to bear his suffering, and offering the consolations of sincere friendship, with a member addressing supplications to the Master of Life to heal the sick man. Once he succumbs, his sorrowful relatives beg Houackanda to place him among the brave and the good.

Believing the dead make a journey to the other side of the great river—if it pleases the Master of Life—to dwell in a land of eternal sunshine, they place the deceased, dressed in his warrior garments, on planks in the middle of a small wooden shed covered with earth and set near him his weapons and some food. For six weeks to two months, people come to mourn at this sepulcher and to pray for the Master of Life to take notice of the virtues of the deceased. Such is the way of burying people of high rank and illustrious or rich men. As for others, wrapped in a wool blanket or some sort of shroud, they are placed in a grave six feet deep. The form of funereal monuments varies greatly. They can be veritable stone pyramids, although those of which we spoke at the beginning of this work go back to a distant epoch and attest to the presence in this country of a civilized and learned people.

Let us conclude this chapter about mourning with a word about the recent discovery of tombs of Pygmies[32] in the State of Missouri on the banks of the Meramec River near St. Louis. In a cemetery

---

32. The French text is "*tombeaux de Pygmées, dans les Etats de Massachuset's* [*sic*]." We corrected the obvious errors in the phrase, mistakes coming from either Vissier or the printer. As for skeletal remains of Pygmies, in 1818 an uneducated rural man living near the Meramec River fifteen miles southwest of St. Louis, in what today is Fenton, Missouri, accidentally unearthed several stone box graves of prehistoric Indians. Because bones in such interments are often deliberately disarticulated to fit in the small "boxes," he assumed the thousand-year-old skeletons to be those of a diminutive race. The following year, Thomas Say, the zoologist of the Stephen Long expedition, excavated several graves at the site and discounted the Pygmy interpretation. Despite Say's pronouncement, settlement in the area was for a time called Lilliput, a reference to the fictional, tiny people in Jonathan Swift's *Gulliver's Travels*. See Edwin James's 1823 *Account of an Expedition from Pittsburgh to the Rocky Mountains*.

containing many graves, the largest not more than four feet long, there are skeletons from twenty to thirty inches [in length], with big heads disproportionate to the body; the bones are thin, and the teeth are those of mature men. If you want to obtain curious and detailed information about this valuable discovery, open the *Journal des Voyages* to Volume 2, p. 243.

CHAPTER FIFTEEN

Religion

This chapter is the most important of all because it traces the outward relations of the Osages with the Divinity and reveals their beliefs. In the history of a civilized people, such an account would doubtless be one of the longest and of the highest interest. For the history of a tribe of savages, it will strongly recommend itself to the philosopher's meditation; however, disengaged from all metaphysical discourse and reduced to the simple listing of historical facts about worship—details already partially presented—this account will be succinct.

The Osages believe in God, whom they worship under the name Houackanda, here translated as the Master of Life. This name given to the Divinity would seem to indicate that the Osages are materialists and that their God, charged solely with presiding over the actions of men in this world, no longer watches over them once they have gone to the grave. Nothing is more false. The Osages believe in a future life, and, without having a precise understanding of it, they assume the righteous man receives in the next world recompense for his virtues, and the wicked one is punished.

For these savages, death is therefore only the sign of passage over the great river to the other shore, where the noble warrior, the intrepid hunter, and the righteous man are received by the great Houackanda into a delightful land to enjoy all possible happiness. The wicked one, on the contrary, crossing this river is thrown back by storms and sees his vessel broken upon the bank he departed from, and he is condemned to wander those shores in a miserable eternity of sorrow and suffering.

We believe we should transcribe here a passage from the narrative of Mr. Hunter [33] recounting his impression of the Pacific Ocean south of the Columbia River, which the American savages consider to be the separation between the residence of the Master of Life from the

---

33. In his *Memoirs of a Captivity*, Hunter writes that after being orphaned at an unspecified early age, he was taken by Kickapoos; later, over many months, he was passed on to several other tribes before at last ending up with the Grand Osage, then residing in southeast Kansas. When he was about twenty, he left the tribe and placed himself in school, where he says he learned (or relearned) English. In 1824, the year following the first publication of his book, initially titled *Manners and Customs of Several Indian Tribes Located West of the Mississippi*, he traveled to London (and later Paris), where three augmented and re-titled English versions of his *Manners and Customs* appeared and created considerable interest, in no small way because of the humanitarian and Christian-slanted view toward Indians he offered. But upon his return to the United States, his book was widely assailed as a piece of fiction, if not outright fakery, not so much for its details of Indian ways as for Hunter's entwined personal story. Influential men such as William Clark, Lewis Cass, and August Chouteau decried the veracity of many aspects of Hunter's narrative. Nicolas Perrin writes in his review: "The first announcement of the publication of this book found everyone inclined to believe that it came from the pen of some skilled charlatan. But Mr. Hunter's appearance in England, supplied with letters of recommendation from the most honorable people of the United States, was enough to dissipate all suspicions" (66).

For charges against Hunter by a contemporary, see the anonymous 1826 review in the *North American Review* listed in the Bibliography.

He went to Texas to join a group trying to ameliorate American attitudes toward and practices against Indians; part of the plan of the so-called Fredonians was to establish a buffer state for Natives dispossessed by expansion of the United States. This most contentious issue led to his being murdered, ironically, by an Indian in 1827, the year the six Osages arrived in Paris. Our view, given the implausibility of some of Hunter's autobiography, is that he fabricated a personal story to interweave into his details of Indian "manners and customs." Captivity tales had a long run of popularity in the United States and provided a convenient framework for his progressive, humanitarian, and Christianized view of Indians. Such an approach, in conflict with the widespread removal of tribal Americans from their Native grounds, was a manifest threat to unchallenged expansion. For more on this view, see Richard Drinnon's 1972 study, *White Savage: The Case of John Dunn Hunter*. The passage Vissier cites is one of the most problematic in Hunter's *Memoirs*. See note 9 to *Six Red Indians*.

temporary abode of his red children. Hunter is quoted in the *Journal des Voyages*, Volume 24, p. 56: "We contemplated with silent dread the numerous difficulties over which we should be obliged to triumph after death, before we could arrive at the delightful hunting grounds reserved for those alone who have done good and loved the Great Spirit. In vain we looked for the broken and sunken canoes of those who did evil, and we were unable to perceive any which made us hope they were few in number."[34]

These crude notions about the afterlife, as mistaken as they are, incontestably prove that the savages of North America believe in the immortality of the soul and in a God of rewards and punishments. As with almost all peoples, they also believe in the demon of evil, whose fatal power they fear, and invoke him in terror: that they may more surely succeed in disarming him, they pray for the Master of Life to be favorable to them.

Their worship is as simple as their ideas. They beseech God every time they need his protection for the success of an enterprise, whether in going to war or the hunt, as well as during sickness of relatives; every five days they appeal to him for their general needs, their prayer made while standing, head lifted towards Heaven. Here is the way they appeal for help: "Oh Master of Life, in Thee I place all my hope! Accord me Thy divine protection in all my undertakings. May my hunt be abundant, may I avenge my country for the outrages of our enemies, and may my might triumph over the murderers of my father, my wives, my children, and those of my compatriot brothers. It is Thou, all powerful Master of Life, whom I implore. Men, weak like me, can do nothing except through Thee, for they can only lend me a hand."

At the time of sowing corn, the women's task is also to address a special prayer to the Master of Life. Mornings, at sunrise for five consecutive days, the women come out of their domiciles with a small quantity of corn to speak the following prayer to the Master of Life: "Here is the time of putting our grain into the earth. May the harvest be abundant. Make fertile the grain I offer Thee, and give

---

34. This quotation comes directly from Perrin's review of the *Memoirs*. See note 9 to *Six Red Indians*.

it power to become bountiful along with all that I will sow with it." After these five days of prayer, the women put the kernels enriched by the Master of Life in with those they are going to sow and mix them together for five days; then, certain of an abundant harvest, they entrust them to the earth. This ceremony, having similarities to the festivals of Ceres,[35] is performed in the presence of a juggler. To address God, women take off their clothes.

Priests—if we can identify without profaning a saintly title the sorry jugglers, those skillful imposters—we may say in certainty are not what a simple people believe them to be. The credulity of believers is at the heart of all their knowledge, for jugglers are not intermediaries between man and the Divinity in this ceremony because each person in that savage country directly addresses his vows to the sky. The service of jugglers is reduced to explaining dreams and predicting the future, but only for events in this life: They never meddle with prejudgments about eternal life.

An Osage, very superstitious, believes in ghosts, but he never sees them except when alone at night when he may often run back to the lodge as quickly as possible, crying out in terror at the idea of the phantom he believes is chasing him. This apparition is always a frightening augury he hastens to tell the juggler, who either calms the fear or augments it, according to what his own interest requires.

CHAPTER SIXTEEN

Miscellaneous Items

The Osages excel in preparing pelts, tanning hides, and in leather work. Furs being their only commercial article, they prepare them perfectly. They also practice the art of coloring mats in a bright, varied, and durable way.

———

35. The ancient Roman mythological figure was honored with several celebrations; the one alluded to here relates to her role as a goddess of cereal grains.

Being heavy smokers, they cultivate tobacco and make clay pipes as well as other crude pottery.

======

They are hospitable, as we have said, and we offer proof in recounting an event recorded in Volume 24, p. 72, of the *Journal des Voyages.*

The Osages were at war with the Kanzas;[36] several savages from the latter tribe, far from their village, realized the impossibility of defending themselves against numerous war parties scouring the country in all directions and resolved to place themselves under the protection of their enemies by sending two emissaries to them. This action of the Kanzas is the highest praise one could make of the reputation the Osages have in the minds of their rivals. Upon the approach of these two heralds of peace, the chief of the Osages assembled his council, and soon a deputation of ten warriors left to announce to the Kanzas they would receive a brotherly welcome. Upon their arrival, the first conference with the chief of the Osages was filled with nobility and worthy of the greatest diplomats of civilized nations: "Our tribes are at war," said Kynistah, chief of the Kanzas. "Several moons ago, on my departure for the hunt, I left them in peace. We had no hostile intentions towards your tribe. Now I cannot go back to my lands safely, and I have come to rest in yours and to ask for hospitality."

It was like this in 1815 when a defenseless Napoleon[37] put his trust in the generosity of the English, who, more maliciously destructive than the savages, betrayed his trust, took advantage of his weakness, and covered themselves with a shame that will resound throughout centuries and will mark that government with the stamp of disloyalty without parallel in history.

The chief of the Osages extended a welcoming hand to his defenseless enemy and gave him assurance of his protection and consider-

---

36. This tribe was once part of the Osages. Vissier's idealistic statement about the reputation of Osage warriors among their rivals would not find accord from many other tribes—certainly not the Pawnees.

37. After his defeat at Waterloo in 1815, the emperor, deprived of his army, was exiled to a remote Atlantic island, Saint Helena, under English supervision. Another example of Vissier using the Osage visit to give his comments on contemporary issues.

ation by inviting the Kanzas to sit at his fire and smoke the pipe with his brothers. In all lodges these guests received a generous reception and everywhere were also accorded the most touching hospitality.

=====

A gross error represents these men as anthropophagi. The truth is they never eat raw meat; on the contrary, they cook it longer than that served on our tables, and, they even more than we, abhor human flesh. We can mention only one man, blinded by frenzied hate, who bit into the heart of his enemy in an act of atrocious barbarism, something not without example among civilized peoples when they are prey to the horrors of civil war.

=====

We earlier said the Osages are illiterate, but that does not mean other tribes of North America do not have a few extraordinary savants who know how to read and write. The author of the brochure printed in Le Havre states on page 21 [p. 55]: "Alphabetical charac-ters *being unknown*, ALL (the savages of North America) use hiero-glyphic symbols; they inscribe their correspondence and all items which must be remembered on the interior bark of the white birch (*Betula papyracea*), or on skins prepared for this purpose. Stylets of iron, wood, or stone, or brushes made of hair, feathers, or wood fibers are the instruments used to draw or paint the most prominent fea-tures of the subject they are trying to convey: the imagination of the reader must supply the rest." This estimable author, who never indi-cates the sources[38] from which he draws, makes it impossible for us to appraise the merit of this assertion. We can, however, with assurance maintain he has been ill informed because this brief passage contains two grave errors: the first, that characters of writing are unknown in North America, and the second, that *all* the inhabitants of this vast country are artisans who possess the skill of reproducing with the

---

38. In the second edition of *Six Red Indians*, Hunter is cited three times by name, but the author makes no mention of Perrin's review of *Memoirs* in the *Journal des Voyages*. Although Vissier does identify some of his sources, he casti-gates the author of *Six Red Indians* for failing to do so; yet he takes this passage directly from Perrin without acknowledgment.

help of a brush images which they wish to commit to memory. This last assertion disproves itself by itself.

As for the first assertion, it is disproved by the following anecdote found in the *Journal des Voyages*, Volume 13, p. 391, to wit: "Captain Douglas has brought to London, from the shores of the Mississippi, a very remarkable curiosity: it is a letter written in 1820, by the Chippewa Indian tribe, and addressed to the Sioux, along with the reply from the latter. *It is written* [Vissier's emphasis] on birch bark, with the point of a knife or some pointed instrument. This *writing* is symbolic or hieroglyphic, and shows how the Indians of North America communicate their ideas with each other today. We ourselves possess an exceptional example of this sort, a letter engraved on bark and perfectly written."

CHAPTER SEVENTEEN

Journey of the Six Osages to Europe

The Osages, a tribe so eminently warlike, profess to the highest degree a feeling of admiration for the French nation, whose military glory has for so long resounded in their ears. From neighbors of St. Louis and New Orleans, with whom they have frequent connections, the inquisitive Osages have often heard exalted the glory of our armies. They learned that our soldiers contributed to the emancipation of the United States, which they consider their mother country. Hence their enthusiasm for the French, whom they believe to be a people like demigods,[39] a nation nothing can resist. Such are the determining causes of the journey that the six Osages we have among us had been considering for several years.

---

39. On a visit to Washington City, one of the well-known Osage chiefs, the first White Hair, or Pawhuska (Paw-Hiu-Skah), speaking for the tribe in 1804 in the initial year of American hegemony in Osage territory, said to President Thomas Jefferson, "I have come with my head down, I hope to return with it raised. I have long since been sold as Negroes are sold. I hope that is done, and that we shall not have to at all times await petty Frenchmen coming to our villages to give bad counsel" (quoted in Foley and Rice, *American West*, 8).

They gathered together, at first some twenty-five, to visit the chief of white warriors (the king of France), their First Father, and they hunted [game] for four years in order to fund this pleasure trip, but death and solicitations of families reduced that number to twelve. Enabled by the gains of their four years of hunting, in 1827 the remainder descended the Missouri on rafts carrying furs to their First Father, as well as the funds produced by the sale of other pelts—intended to cover expenses of the voyage, and finally their arms and clothes.

Heaven, which so often enjoys upsetting the plans of men, did not grant the twelve Osages safe arrival in port. Near St. Louis their raft capsized and the waters engulfed furs, money, arms, and baggage. Our travelers are still grateful for being able to swim to shore and to arrive naked but alive in the city of St. Louis. This deplorable event almost constrained them to give up their project, but the savages persevered. They knew in St. Louis a warrior who they often saw bearing arms, a leader of his brothers. For a long time this military man had earned their confidence with his bravery and his humanity; moreover, they knew this chief of white warriors is French and planned to make a journey to his own tribe, so they asked him to lead them.

But no longer do they have[40] any gifts to offer to their First Father! No matter! They will tell him they had some, but the waters swallowed them, and the king will not doubt them because he knows they never lie. They have no money to provide for sustenance, but their First Father will provide it; the chief of the Tribe of the French surely will be generous and hospitable. They are determined to go there, so they convince a ship owner to grant them passage on a big fireboat. Nothing will keep them from going.

At the moment of departure, however, six of them recoiled at the thought of the perils of the [ocean] crossing and gave up the journey, but those remaining, four men and two women, embarked under the auspices of Mr. David Delaunay, native of France, for twenty-seven years an inhabitant of St. Louis, and a colonel in the service of the

---

40. Vissier shifts briefly to the present tense to dramatize this past event.

United States. With them embarked Mr. Tesson, their guide, also an inhabitant of St. Louis, and Mr. Paul Loise, their interpreter, born of a Frenchman and an Osage woman; still in touch with their tribe, he speaks their language and has all their affection. They proceeded down the Mississippi on a steamboat named *Commerce* to reach New Orleans, their place of departure for the great voyage. After a happy passage of five hundred leagues, they arrived in the capital of Louisiana and were favorably welcomed as they prepared themselves to embark on the great crossing.

Before setting foot on the ship to transport them to the Tribe of the French, they paused and again contemplated the immense waters of the ocean. Marcharthiahtoongah, forty-five years old, called "The Orator," addressed the ocean in these terms: "Thou, Water, dost think to frighten us? No! We left our village to visit our brothers, the French, and all peoples on the other side of the great lake. Death alone can prevent us from making this journey." Following his brief allocution, they embarked on the American ship, the *New-England*, under the command of Captain Hunt. After a long and difficult crossing, they arrived 27 July 1827 at Le Havre at the mouth of the Seine.

It would be difficult to say which was greater, the curiosity of the North American savages, landing for the first time in a European port among a people of whom they have such an extraordinary idea, or the curiosity of the French at the arrival of six savage redskins. To judge by the eagerness and number of spectators at the debarkation of the Osages, one would be tempted to believe that among us curiosity was even greater than among those who had made many sacrifices in order to visit us.

The crowd was large on the wharf, in the rigging, and on the masts and spars of ships near the one just arrived. In order to protect their debarkation from the crush of the multitude surrounding them with impulsive eagerness that could have caused injuries, the authorities were obliged to use military force in order to open a passage from the ship to the carriage waiting on the wharf. The hotel the Osages were conducted to was immediately assailed. There the Indians needed several days of rest before continuing their journey toward the capital [Paris]. Only after presenting themselves at a theatre much too small, only after having visited all the authorities and notable personages of Le Havre, and only after having often ridden around in an open carriage in all quarters of the city were they able to enter a vehicle without the intervention of a protective escort.

Their costumes, their weapons, the color of their copper-red skin, and the beauty and regularity of their impassive features—each thing about them was a surprise. Everyone tried to approach them, to touch their hands, and to obtain from them a gracious gesture full of nobility. They were invited to the homes of the most important businessmen, who feted them in the city and in the country; ladies gave the two savage women objects from their toilette: buckles, belts, bracelets, fans, earrings, garters, rings, necklaces, etcetera—all of it accepted with an eagerness equal to that with which it was offered. The four men, although somewhat short for Osages, are from five feet four inches to five feet five inches tall,[41] and the women proportionally smaller, at the most five feet tall.

Fatigued by so many parties and dazzled by so many things, they longed for moments of solitude when they could gather together to

------

41. After meeting in a delegation of Osage chiefs in Washington City, President Jefferson proclaimed them "the finest men we have ever seen." Indeed, many early travelers and traders commented on the impressive height of Osage warriors. In the 1820s, Paul Wilhelm wrote in his *Travels in North America:* "The Osages have the reputation of being the tallest and strongest Indians in the western territory. Even though their giant size may be greatly exaggerated, I cannot deny that all the individuals of this nation that I had an opportunity to see were very strong and muscularly built," (195).

A decade later, in his *Letters and Notes*, George Catlin said: "The Osages may justly be said to be the tallest race of men in North America, either of red or white skins; there being very few indeed of the men, at their full growth, who are less than six feet in stature, and very many of them six and a half, and others seven feet. They are at the same time well-proportioned in their limbs, and good-looking," (Vol. 2, 40).

In 1974, a full-blood, six-foot-four-inch Osage man whose last name was Tall Chief said to William Least Heat-Moon, "People used to call us the giants of the prairies because in another time when our warriors won a battle, we would rub out the tallest of the enemy and carry off to our villages the tallest of their children. What can I say? I probably have some Pawnee blood."

recapitulate the events of the day and those of the day before in order to arrange them in their memory and recount them later to their compatriots. The most simple things caught their attention: A small dog playing in the street with another dog, an old, deformed woman, and a legless person were the initial objects of their interest. Little accustomed to seeing such physical defects at home, the first time they noticed a legless man, they asked if there was a tribe so disfavored by nature.

On August 7, they embarked on a steamboat at six in the morning to go to Rouen, where the crowd, waiting four days for them, rushed to the wharf upon arrival of the boat from Le Havre. To avoid accidents mobs of the curious in their eagerness might occasion, the Osages debarked one league away from the city for waiting carriages to take them to the hotel. In their new quarters, they became the object of the same attention as in Le Havre, causing crowds to run after them everywhere. Finally arriving in Paris on August 13, they stopped at the Terrace Hotel, rue de Rivoli.[42] There, as in Rouen, public curiosity was disappointed: although unable to see them, a great throng of the curious gathered in front of this hotel. Having come from so far away in order to greet the chief of the French warriors, their First Father, the Osages wanted to conform to the custom requiring a foreigner initially to call upon the chief of the Tribe.

Unfortunately, their eagerness to present their respectful homage to the sovereign of the French could not be satisfied as quickly as they would have liked because court etiquette and social convention opposed it; it was only on 21 August 1827 at eleven in the morning, they were able at last to be presented to the king in his chateau at Saint-Cloud.[43]

Receiving them with all the kindness of a tender father, his Maj-

---

42. A major thoroughfare in the center of Paris and paralleling the Seine.

43. It was a signal honor to be received personally by the king in his main country residence, and to be introduced to his family, including the so-called "Children of France." The six Osages were accorded honors normally reserved for ambassadors and other dignitaries. The reception, coming only about three weeks after the arrival of the Osages in France, must have given Delaunay much hope for the success of his venture.

esty told the chief he was happy to see him and said that *the Osage tribe had always been faithful to France while their country was under its domination, and that he hoped the Osages would be equally faithful allies of the United States.*

His Majesty then spoke to Mr. David Delaunay to express his satisfaction with the arrival and visit of the savages. Madame the Duchess of Angoulême[44] granted them the favor of letting them see the Children of France, while speaking to the Osage chief with most obliging words. The chief delivered the following speech to the king: "My Great Sovereign, in my childhood, I heard my father speak of the French nation. I formed then the idea of seeing it when I was grown. I became a man, and I am accomplishing my desire. I am today, with those who accompany me, among the French we love so much, and I have the pleasure of being in the presence of their king. We salute France."

After His Majesty retired, the Osages were led to rooms in the chateau and then brought into the salon of the Marshal Duke de Bellune,[45] who received them with all possible affability. Several ladies of the court were there. Following refreshments and having spent about one and a half hours in the chateau, the Osages left for Paris.

CHAPTER EIGHTEEN

Historical Notice on Each of the Osages

The most distinguished of the six Osages among us is a prince of blood of the reigning dynasty. Named Kishagashugah, he is thirty-six years old and chief of a village; his wife and one of her cousins

---

44. Marie-Therese of France, daughter of Louis XVI, survived the Revolution and married the son of Charles X. In other words, the king passed along some of the duties of a state reception for the Osages to his daughter-in-law, who in turn presented his direct descendants, the "Children of France." Coincidentally, the steamboat carrying the Osages from Le Havre to Rouen bore her name.

45. An honored military man whose career extended from the Revolution to Napoleon.

accompany him. The princess, eighteen years old, is named Myhan-gah. Her cousin, nineteen years old, is Gretomih. They are both attractive women, with handsome black eyes, their skin more olive than copper. An ancestor of this minor chief of the Osage tribe came to France during the reign of Louis XIV,[46] whom he saw, and from whom he received a most distinguished welcome. Flattered by the graceful reception that the monarch accorded him and by the way which, in imitation of the king, all the gentlemen of the court welcomed him, as well as the welcome from authorities and inhabitants of France whom he met, he took back home the enthusiasm he had developed for the French nation.

The author of the brochure printed in Le Havre states on page 27 [pp. 59–60] that upon the chief's return from the journey to the court of Louis XIV, the Osage traveler called together his tribe and gave an account of his voyage. The author further says that "upon hearing this account the present chief" (the one now in France and to whom he attributes the age of thirty-eight) exclaimed: "And I too will visit France if the Master of Life permits me to become a man."

Our estimable author—who always confounds places, individuals, peoples, and times, spurred on by the desire to publish his book—did not notice that in order to tell this tale at the beginning of the nine-teenth century, the grandfather, surely having come to France as a mature man in the reign of Louis XIV in the seventeenth century, must have been truly old when he inspired his grandson. Convinced that [oral] tradition alone could have revealed to Kishagashugah the voyage of his ancestor, we learned from him that it is in fact thanks to the story of this trip that we owe the visit he has made to us in 1827 along with his wife, her cousin, and three distinguished warriors of his tribe.

One of these three warriors, Washingasbha, called "Black Spirit," is illustrious among the Osages, thanks to the number of enemies he has felled. The second chief of the village, which the prince com-

---

46. The second edition of *Six Red Indians* is the only one naming Louis XIV as the monarch who greeted the first Osage to visit the royal court in 1725. See the first note to our introduction and note 41 to *Six Red Indians*.

mands, has taken five scalps and is honored by his exploits as much as by his distinguished birth.

Marcharthitahtoongah, called The Orator because of his eloquence, at forty-five years old is the oldest of the six and has distinguished himself in the bearing of arms and the taking of three scalps. The youngest, Minckchatahooh, just twenty-six, has scalped but one enemy because he fought in only one campaign.

Such are the six illustrious savages who have come to visit us.

About the Text of

Remarks about the Six Indians

SHORTLY AFTER THE OSAGES arrived in Paris in early August, at least four pamphlets appeared with almost identical titles beginning with the word *Notice* ("Remarks"). Of them, *Remarks about the Six Indians*, the only one written in the first person, contains significant details not appearing in either *Six Red Indians* or Vissier's *History*. The author, who spent time with the Osages during their stay in Le Havre, not only adds new facts but also confirms many of the more general assertions made in the other two booklets. Despite his continual chauvinism, his point of view and affection for the Indians, as well as his somewhat more lively expression, give his report distinction.

References noted in *Six Red Indians* and Vissier's *History* are not repeated here.

REMARKS

ABOUT

THE SIX INDIANS

Who Arrived in Le Havre

ON THE AMERICAN BRIG NEW-ENGLAND,
JULY 27, 1827,

IN WHICH CAN BE FOUND

THE LITERAL TRANSLATION OF THE

SPEECH DELIVERED BY THEIR CHIEF

TO THE COMMANDANT OF THE CITY,

BY A PERSON WHO WAS

WITH THEM CONTINUALLY.

———————

PARIS,

THE FRENCH AND FOREIGN BOOKSTORE,

PALAIS-ROYAL, GALERIES DE BOIS.

———

1827

Remarks about the Six Indians

PUBLIC CURIOSITY HAS BEEN greatly aroused by the arrival in France of six savage inhabitants from the shores of the Missouri River. I have tried, in order to satisfy this curiosity, to outline a brief sketch of their manners and customs, but the rapidity with which I wrote this account forces me to beg for the reader's indulgence. I have a post in Le Havre, which allowed me to obtain interesting details from the chief of these Indians with the help of his interpreter, Mr. Paul Loise, born of a Frenchman and an Osage woman in Fort Louis, a place located five hundred leagues above New Orleans, to the west of the Mississippi.

On the 27th of July, on the noon high tide, accompanied by Mr. Delaunay, former officer of His Majesty Louis XVI, the following Indians debarked in our port:

Kihegashugah, known as Little Chief, thirty-five years old, a general distinguished by his bravery, of tall stature and well-formed body with muscular limbs, showing strength and agility; he is the second chief of a tribe located some thirty leagues from the Missouri. Waschingsabhe, or Black Spirit, his second in command, age thirty-four, with a good-looking stature; Gretomih, spouse and cousin of Little Chief, age eighteen and one-half; Myhanga, related to Gretomih, age eighteen; Marcharthita-Hatangah, or Big Soldier, age forty-eight; and Minkcha-tagonh, or Little Soldier, age twenty-two.

These individuals speak a guttural language, and their voices are sonorous with their words accompanied by expressive gestures. No other language resembles theirs, which they transmit to their children without the help of books.

Their skin is the color of dark-red copper; they are naked down to the waist with a white wool blanket barely covering the buttocks and thighs. Both chiefs and the soldiers have shaved heads except on the crown where a small tuft of hair is left, which they plait into two braids and there attach silver plaques the length and width of a knife blade. The skin of the head is lightly painted with Chinese red [vermilion]. A handkerchief of silk or wool folded like a cravat is placed around the head and knotted in front just above the forehead. Three ostrich feathers,[1] one black and two white and red, and a few strings of false pearls are used as adornments. On reaching adulthood, they pull out facial hair with tweezers.

Edges of the eyelids and the most prominent parts of cheeks and ears are painted green and red; the lower part of the temples, forehead, and chin are also painted with vermilion (in their language *houassouze*) and a touch of verdigris (*houazetton*),[2] which the Indians get in New Orleans. These crude drawings on the face vary according to the taste of the Indian, who decorates himself only when he wants to be noticed in public.

Osage men and women wear necklaces of false pearls and clay beads, and also an oval, concave medallion—made in the United States—which is suspended from several strands worn around the neck. Both men and women pierce their ears in several places and hang little strands there, which I have already talked about. I have also noticed they keep their fingernails quite long.

Silver bands garnished with little copper bells of a Parisian style decorate the upper arm, and similar bracelets ornament each wrist—all these bijoux are made in New Orleans by French and English goldsmiths.

These Indians wear mitas, a sort of shoe, and high deerskin leggings they fasten near the buttocks; a square piece of red cloth tied in front and in back barely hides the sexual organs.

The two chiefs and their soldiers each carry a little hatchet weapon

---

1. The plumes could have come from several different North American birds, but not from the African ostrich.

2. A green or greenish-blue pigment Indians used for print.

they call *ichin-kigratchi,* or rod of authority.[3] It is a weapon that looks almost like one side of a wooden mule collar. It is painted and decorated with nails with gilded heads, strands of beads, feathers, and bells. This sort of hatchet, made of wood, is not only used as a weapon in the bloody battles they have with other tribes but also is an object of pleasure and display in their hands. This ichin-kigratchi is crossed with a polished iron blade shaped like an elongated heart with some holes in it here and there; the tip is always carried pointing forward by the Osage.

The two young women who accompany the men make themselves noticed by their polite manners; they are of average height, their eyes lively, and their teeth straight. They are bareheaded, with long hair divided in front by a wooden comb in such a way that the scalp is seen in the part which they rub with vermilion every morning. I watched them do this when I visited them. Their laughing and pleasant faces exude sweetness.

Dress of these women consists of a sort of blouse, which does not go below the knee, made of a cotton fabric in the American style; they wear mitas and high leggings of goatskin. A square piece of red wool cloth, attached in front of and behind a small shirt, covers the lower part of the body. A much larger square of cloth, bordered with yellow, red, and white ribbons they made, completes their inexpensive outfits. Their necklaces and four armbands are rather more elegant than the men's.

These Indians from the Little Osage River[4] are deists who worship God as the Master of Life, and every day they address prayers and thanksgiving to him. They have lunar months. Polygamy is permitted among them. I will say nothing certain about their origin because it is surrounded by fable and superstition. They believe that the first of their race came from the shell of a snail,[5] and without reasoning they repeat other such tales, as do all savages who do not have a written history.

---

3. The Boilly and Colson illustrations give an idea of this instrument, which was both a weapon and symbol of position. The Colson illustration also shows a staff.

4. This tributary joins the Osage River in western Missouri.

5. See note 36 to *Six Red Indians.*

Captain Hunt, commander of the ship *New-England*, told me that when they reached the north end of the jetty, some twelve hundred yards from the outer harbor of Le Havre, Black Spirit,[6] whose name is respected among the people of his nation, stood up to address the ocean, just as he did before their departure, and thanked God with great fervor for having granted them a successful voyage.

I will set down here what Little Chief told the Captain a few moments before arriving in Le Havre.

> Under the glorious reign of Louis XIV,[7] my great-grandfather visited France. He was presented to that superb court by an ambassador and received by the monarch with manifestations of true friendship. Afterwards he traveled through the interior of France, where he received the same signs of interest and protection. On his return to western Missouri, in the midst of his family, he shared with them his gratitude to the chief of the French nation and the admiration with which he was struck upon seeing Louis XIV seated on his throne. This sacred memory has perpetuated itself in our family. So I, Kihegashugah, a descendant of that happy Indian, have chosen the year 1827 to undertake this great and perilous journey which some warriors under my command strongly opposed.

At one o'clock the debarkation took place, and the Osages got into two rented carriages that took them to the Hotel Holland for lunch. At four o'clock, in these same carriages (which they would use until their departure for Paris), along with M. Delaunay and Mr. Paul Loise, their official interpreter, they went to call upon the mayor of Le Havre who has a house on the Ingouville coast.[8] They were welcomed by that respectable magistrate who for refreshment offered them some red wine from Bordeaux. After tasting it, they refused more, so they were offered some sweet white wines, and they drank

---

6. Other texts give the speaker as Big Soldier, or The Orator, one more likely to offer a prayer.

7. See note 1 to the introduction.

8. In 1827 this seaside village lay just outside Le Havre before being incorporated into the city in the mid-nineteenth century.

with great pleasure some muscatel from Rivesaltes (Roussillon). However, two glasses of this wine downed one right after the other by Big Soldier upset him to the point of provoking vomiting.

Afterwards the Osages walked around a nicely planted park. They had barely gone fifty steps when Black Spirit, upon seeing a handsome Carolina poplar (Florida),⁹ opened his arms, warmly approached Little Chief, and said: "Warrior, look at this tree from our country." Enchanted with everything around them, they went back to the hotel, on rue Saint-Julien, where Mr. and Mrs. Dupres were unstinting in their attention to them.

The next day, the 28th, all of them, except for Big Soldier who was retained at the hotel by an indisposition, went to the Headquarters office to ask for the honor of being presented to the king's representative, who hastened to receive them, showing them every consideration. I was placed near the colonel, four steps away from the Indians, while dignitaries from town were grouped behind us. Then Little Chief, Kihegashugah, stood, bowed, and in a guttural voice, accompanied by gestures, addressed to the commander of the commune these words, which the interpreter assures me he has faithfully translated:

My friend! If I permit myself to call you my friend, it is because I am your equal. You, your officers, and all these people here prove to me that you are highly respected. I too am a chief, a fearsome warrior in my own country, which is so far away from yours! However, I would be deceitful if I told you I was the supreme chief of my country. I am only a subordinate chief. The great chiefs of the country have stayed there in order to govern the people, who in time of peace think only about hunting animals which can harm people. These animals, whose pelts we sell to white men living on the other side of the ocean (the Europeans), are the tiger, white bear, wolf, fox, and others. For our daily nourishment we hunt wild cattle, cows,¹⁰ roe deer, hinds, stags, and others.

---

9. It's unclear what the author intends by the parenthetical.

10. The animals are probably the grizzly, bison, and feral beef or dairy cows.

My worthy compatriots became sad upon my departure. Here is Waschingsabhe; he is a warrior, a skillful hunter. He has five scalps taken from enemies he has killed. This is my wife and cousin, Gretomih, and Myhanga, a relative. That man there is Little Soldier, Minkcha-Tagonh. He is a most agile runner. He is brave and at his young age he already has two scalps of enemies felled by his blows.

Having heard my grandfather speak of the French people, of their kindness, of their ancient glory, and of my great-grandfather, chief of the Osages, who expressed his ardent wish that a descendant of his visit this France so rich in products and historic actions, even as a child, I told my family that if God protected my life, I would go to France accompanied by relatives. Now here I am before you.

I am expecting news from Paris, and before long I will go see my grandfather (the Indian meant he will go see His Majesty Charles X). I will ask him to take care of me, and in twelve moons (one year) I will take back to the Natives of my country impressions of all I do and see in the king's palace, he who commands a people whose renown has given me a memory of kindness, richness, and courage.[11]

After this speech he sat down, then again standing suddenly, he extended his hand to me and said: "My friend, my highest ambition is to see myself dressed like you, to carry a beautiful sword like yours, and to have those beautiful golden fringes on my shoulders."

The sweetness and desire these Indians manifest to learn from us and the signs of pleasure exhibited when they find themselves being treated politely make us hope to see them spend some time in Europe. It would be easy to civilize such people to bring them out of the savage state in which nature still holds them. The manners of

---

11. The author here includes a footnote:

Mr. Delaunay—a former officer and a man rightfully respected, who has the confidence of the six Osages—and Mr. Paul Loise have both assured me that these Indians from northwestern America have made progress towards civilization in the last half century and that they are aware of current events in Asia and Europe.

these Osages, which I could contrast with those of some Cossacks and Tartars I saw on an immense field, have left a pleasant impression on my mind, one to last a long time.

Upon leaving the king's representative, they went to see the town authorities.

That evening at seven o'clock, at the insistence of the stage manager, they attended the theater. The heat was overwhelming and the crowd large. An opera by Monvel, *Blaise and Babet*,[12] was to be performed, and Potier was supposed to appear on the stage that evening. Although when the curtain was raised, all attention and glances were directed towards the Indians, and the lovely music of the famous composer from Liège was neglected.

The Osages were given refreshing drinks of orgeat[13] and currant syrup, which they much enjoyed. Their emotion was visible when the lord of the manor, Mr. de Belval, takes Blaise and Babet under his protection and brings them back together, and when Grandfather Mathurin, Mr. de Belval's tenant farmer, receives bouquets for his birthday from his children and village people. But deafened by the whispering and brouhaha that always happen in large crowds, and suffocated by the heat made more intense because of the growing throng, the Osages left without hearing any of the numbers Potier was scheduled to perform.

On Sunday the 29th, at eleven in the morning, I invited the Indians to visit the citadel to see the parade. They agreed to come, except for Big Soldier, still indisposed. Upon my arrival at their hotel I underwent a rigorous inspection; I had to let them touch my medals and my sword, and demonstrate its use as a weapon.

I got into an open carriage with Little Chief, the two women, and the interpreter. The second chief, the young soldier, Mr. Delaunay, and Mr. Tesson of New Orleans followed in another carriage. All of Le Havre was lined up on the route. The lovely Myhanga (she must be so considered in her country), pressing herself against me, seemed to show some fear of the ever-growing crowd. I explained to

---

12. See notes 45 and 47 to *Six Red Indians*.

13. A sweet beverage made from barley and oranges with almonds sometimes added.

her that French people, even though they were kind and generous, were also most inquisitive, especially in such circumstances, and that they experienced a great joy, a veritable need to admire the Indians. I told them I had heard some sailors, many of whom had gone up the Missouri on steamboats, say that the Osages were mild mannered, hospitable, and excellent hunters. Hearing these remarks, the Indians bowed to the right and to the left in order to salute the inhabitants of Le Havre, and once again the Osages shook my hand.

Arriving at the citadel, they showed astonishment at the handsome uniforms of the officers and soldiers, the maneuvers, the drums, and the music—especially the trumpets—all of it seeming to interest them.

On the 30th they were feted during a meal with a rich country proprietor. On the 31st, they went on an outing at Ingouville. On the 1st of August, at six in the evening, the Osages went to the riding school, where they often applauded the agility and grace the French displayed on horseback. At seven-thirty they attended the little Ingouville theater to watch with delight some dances on a tightrope and a comic pantomime performed expressly for them.

For my part, anxious to show off my nation, I never failed to call their attention to whatever might please them or arouse their curiosity. I pointed out the splendor of the throne, the kindness of the king, the riches of the merchants of one of the most beautiful capitals of the world,[14] the extraordinary beauty of many buildings that embellish this stunning city, and the order, politeness, and trust existing among the citizens. When I had finished sketching out this incomplete picture, Little Chief, whom I was next to at the theater, said to me: "My friend, when I left Fort Louis, my mind was full of seductive illusions, which have been changed every day into realities because of things I am seeing. I am glad to see I was not wrong about the French, and I thank God for that."

---

14. Although the placement of this sentence makes it appear to be about Le Havre, it is rather about Paris. With his usual chauvinism, the author interjects his preparing the Osages for their anticipated visit to the capital.

At nine o'clock they returned to the hotel and invited me to supper. Although I was not hungry, I immediately accepted because I wanted to profit from the occasion to study their customs. They placed themselves on the same side of the table. I was seated across from them, with Mr. Delaunay on my right and Mr. Loise on my left. There was a moment of complete silence during which they kept their eyes lowered. Waiters served beefsteaks and veal, with all the meats cooked well done. The Osages ate a good deal, especially Big Soldier, who from time to time would pat his dark and naked belly and exclaim: *"Ah! How full it is getting with all these good things from white men!"*

When the omelet was served, they mixed it with different pieces of meat and ate it all together; then they drank a cup of bouillon and some water before eating more meat with a little bread, and then finished the meal with fruit and tea. These Indians have a decided taste for cooked meat, which proves they are not cannibals.

That night at ten o'clock, wanting to give me a treat, they agreed to sing. All four sat on a bench. A short-handled gourd filled with little rocks was used to beat the rhythm and provide accompaniment. They finished with a solemn song in honor of God.

On the 2nd, another outing at Ingouville. On the 3rd, the Osages attended a big fencing demonstration at the merchants hall. From childhood on they are accustomed to bodily exercise, such as running, riding horseback, swimming, and using firearms or knives, but their enthusiasm burst forth upon seeing the fencing masters who took part in the demonstration. The Indians touched the foils and tried to imitate those who had just been using them.

On the [4th], they took an excursion to the countryside. On the 5th, a Sunday, Big Soldier, now recovered from his weariness and indigestion caused by eating too much fruit, promised to go to town with Little Chief. At two in the afternoon we took them to see Mr. Belot, a doctor and physiologist who had invited several people to his place to witness a physics demonstration using an electric machine. Little Chief received several sparks on the back of his hand when he stuck it into the device conducting the electricity.

Black Spirit also consented to receive an electrical charge, but Big Soldier, somewhat afraid, begged off even though Little Chief and his compatriots laughed at him. Several other amusing tricks of physics were performed, and then the physics lesson came back to electricity with Volta's spark gun. Little Chief, Black Spirit, and Big Soldier held hands to form a chain; then Little Chief went to get a spark from the Leyden jar. The jolt was much stronger this time because the device had been set to produce a greater shock. In a repeat of the experiment, the two women held hands with the men; then Kihegashugah asked Mr. Belot to let the ladies from Le Havre, who filled most of the seats in the hall, take part in these amusements. Some of them refused but many got in on the game by extending their hands in friendship to the Osages who on this occasion once again realized how people were showing them kindness and confidence. Then Little Chief went one more time to the machine to receive a charge. At the moment of the jolt, the Osages, hearing the French ladies give out the same cry of surprise the shock provoked in themselves, began laughing and said: "Ladies, you also got hit."

Our dignified and learned professor, delighted to have pleased the Indians, asked Little Chief what he thought of the experiments. The Osage replied he had been amazed, although once in Philadelphia[15] he had been taken to an amphitheater holding more than four hundred people, and there had experienced the same effects. While these experiences were not new to him, he affectionately thanked the good doctor, praised the gracious manners of our lovely French women, and was pleased to have attended such a gathering.

On the 6th they did not go out, spending the day packing their trunks and packages.

[While in Le Havre] the cavalry maneuvers [at the citadel], the cannon shots, and the instructive exercises of Mr. Franconi aroused their interest more than anything.

On the 7th, at five o'clock in the morning, the Osages embarked on the steamboat *Duchesse d'Angoulême* and set off for Rouen where

---

15. Probably a reference to the 1806 Osage journey to Washington and other eastern cities.

more than 40,000 curious people were waiting for them, a crowd lining the banks of the Seine for two hours in order to see their arrival.

I am certain the Indians will be in Rouen for four or five days and on the 14th will be in Paris which they are eager to see.

Such are the events I have recorded and such is an exact account of the stay in Le Havre of these "savages," if one can thus label these people who, in truth, are ignorant[16] but who nonetheless obey laws, practice a religion, and are kind and charitable.

------

16. The intended meaning is something like "untutored in the ways of Western Europeans."

Appendix A

Chronology of the Osage Tour

1827

April	Depart Osage villages for St. Louis.
April 29	Osage travelers arrive in St. Louis.
c. May 21	Depart St. Louis for New Orleans.
May 29	Depart New Orleans for Le Havre, France.
July 27	Arrive in Le Havre.
August 1	Copyright date on *Six Indiens Rouges*, 2nd edition.
August 7	Depart Le Havre for Rouen.
August 11	Announcement in *Bibliographie de la France* of publication of *Six Indiens Rouges*, 3rd edition.
August 13	Osages arrive in Paris.
August 19	Osages breakfast with Minister of Foreign Affairs and forty curious guests.
August 21	Osages received by King Charles X at Saint Cloud.
August 22	Announcement in *Bibliographie* of publication of three pamphlets about the Osages, including *Remarks* translated here.
August 25	Announcement in *Bibliographie* of a fourth pamphlet and *Six Indiens Rouges*, 2nd edition (a delay in news arriving from Le Havre).
September 5	Announcement in *Bibliographie* of publication of *Six Indiens Rouges*, 4th edition and *Histoire de la Tribu des Osages*.
December	Travelers to Belgium (Brussels, Verviers, Ghent).
December 24	In Louvain, Belgium, to see a zoo elephant.

1828

January 1	Return to Brussels.
January 2	Arrive in Ghent, Belgium. Trial of David Delaunay begins the following day.
February 10	Mohongo gives birth to twin daughters.
c. March 18	Osages in Amsterdam, Holland.
Summer	Travel to Germany (Frankfurt-am-Main, Dresden, Berlin); Switzerland (Geneva); and Italy.

1829

January	Travel to Fribourg, Switzerland, and Breslau, Prussia [Poland].
June	Return to France and divide into two groups.
November	One group returns to Paris and the other goes to Montauban, France. Both groups destitute.
13 November	First group departs Le Havre for Norfolk, Virginia.

1830

January	First group arrives in Norfolk.
January	Second group departs Bordeaux for New York City.
March	Second group arrives in New York City and is soon moved to Washington, D.C., to join first group. During time in the capital, Mohongo has her portrait painted by Charles Bird King.
6 May	The four surviving Osages depart Washington for St. Louis by stage and steamboat.
6 June	The travelers leave St. Louis for their Osage villages near the Neosho River in what is today northeast Oklahoma. They are received with honor.

Appendix B

Marquis de Lafayette to William Clark, March 22, 1830

Paris, March 22d 1830

My Dear General

   I am happy in every opportunity to address you, and will avail myself of a request made by the last detachment of osages, two men and a woman who are returning home. They are anxious to be bearers of a recommendatory letter from me to you which I give with great pleasure. They all have been the objects of a white speculation, very unprofitable to the author, and to them a source of vexation and disappointment. They however have seen much, and will have much to say to their red brethren. Upon the whole, when once returned home, they will have treasured many remembrances. The behaviour of these four men and two women has been correct. One of the men, I understand, died on the passage. They every where have found the officers and citizens of the U.S. ready to afford them protection and testimonies of kindness, none more acceptable to them than this letter of recommendation. Remember [me] to family and friends and believe me forever

Your affectionate obliged friend

Lafayette

Appendix C

Paul Wilhelm's Disquisition

About the Text of Paul Wilhelm's Disquisition

PAUL WILHELM, P.v.W., draws upon knowledge gained from travels through the American Middle West during his 1822 to 1824 travels in North America. These paragraphs seem to have been written in response to the arrival of the six Osages in Northern Europe, presumably on their visit to Germany, but the pages contain neither date nor place of publication. Internal evidence suggests Wilhelm penned the disquisition in the summer of 1828, perhaps during the Osage visit to Leipzig. The lone version we have come upon has the appearance of a quality offprint from a book, or it may have been disbound, although the nature of the comment carries the ring of a letter to a periodical. The common terms for the two major village groups, the Great Osage and the Little Osage, refer to the size of the villages, but Wilhelm interprets the adjectives as descriptive of the physical stature of the travelers themselves. Paul Vissier estimated the height of the women at about five feet and the men some six inches taller. In his *Travels in North America*, Wilhelm demonstrates keen interest in the bodily and facial appearance of the various tribes he encountered.

Wilhelm's Disquisition

There is no doubt that the North American Indians who have been traveling Europe for a year indeed belong to the Osage tribe and that they are of entirely pure blood. Nonetheless they do not appear to belong to the Grand band but instead to the Little band of the nation. I made this conclusion from the face formation and small height of these Indians, which indicate the slight difference between the Great and the Little Osages. Among the particular groups of Little Osages that I had the opportunity to see in the state of Missouri, I do not remember having seen any of the Indian warriors who are present here now, at least no proper chief seems to be among them. However, a certain family resemblance by which the Indian tribes distinguish themselves among each other unmistakably caught my eye when I got to look at the quite accurate illustrations.

The Osages do not live along the shores of the Missouri River but on the prairies bordering the Osage River between latitude 36 and 38 degrees north and longitude 93 to 99 degrees west of London. As is generally known, many other nations related to the Osages by language and customs still belong to a main tribe, although the times when they had lived together as one are shrouded in darkness now and live on only as a legend passed along from one Indian generation to the next. The clothing, accessories, and weapons of the Osages who are currently in Germany are not authentic; this is due to the fact that all the possessions they had brought from the prairies have apparently been lost to the Mississippi near St. Louis.

Also, the names of the Indians appear to have been falsely transmitted to the audience. Kishagashuga should probably be called Kahige-schinga or Little Chief (from *Kahige* or *Nika-kahige*, which means "chief" and *schinga*, "little"). Washingasbha seems to be a corruption of the common Indian name Washinga-sabae and does not mean Black Spirit but rather Black Bird (from *Was-hinga*, "bird," and *sa-bae*, "black"). Marcharthitahtoongah could perhaps mean *Macha-pi-sche-tangah*—the English write *toongah*—or Big Evil Tent (from *Macha* or *Tschi*, "leather tent," *pi-sche*, "evil," and *tangah*, "big").

Among the Kanzas who compare with the Osages in terms of their language and names, I know at least one warrior by this name; the French merchants call him *la grande mauvaise loge*. Minckchatahooh or Mika-cha-tah-hooh means the "Raccoon with Good Meat," from *Mika-scha*, "raccoon," and *tah*, "meat."

P. v. W.
[Translated by Olaf Schmidt]

Bibliography

Editions of the Three Primary Pamphlets

Anonymous. *Six Indiens rouges de la Tribu des Grands Osages, arrivés du Missouri au Havre, le 27 Juillet 1827, sur le Navire américain New-England, Cap. Hunt.* Seconde Edition, revue, corrigée et augmentée. Au Havre, Chez S. Faure, [1827].

———. Troisième Edition, revue, corrigée et augmentée de particularités intéressantes sur leur séjour au Havre. Delaunay, Libraire de son Altesse Royale, Madame la Duchesse d'Orléans, Palais-Royal, Paris, 1827.

———. Quatrième Edition, revue, corrigée et augmentée de particularités intéressantes sur leur séjour au Havre. Delaunay, Libraire de son Altesse Royale, Madame la Duchesse d'Orléans, Palais-Royal, Paris, 1827.

———. [Brussels edition], (Cette famille étrange, après s'être offerte pendant quelques jours à la contemplation des curieux de la ville de Bruxelles, visitera apparemment les principales villes du Royaume.) Chez J.-B. Dupon, Imprimeur-Libraire, et chez les principaux Libraires du Royaume, Bruxelles, 1827.

———. *Die Sechs kupferrothen Indianer von dem Stamme der grossen Osagen, welche von dem Missuri den 27 Juli 1827 zu Havre de Grace in Frankreich auf dem amerikanischen Schiffe, New-England, Capitain Hunt, angelangt sind.* Nach dem Französischen der dritten vermehrkten und verbesserten Ausgabe. Mit 1 Abbildung. Leipzig, 1827.

Vissier, Paul. *Histoire de la Tribu des Osages, Peuplade sauvage de l'Amérique septentrionale, dans l'Etat du Missouri, l'un des Etats-Unis d'Amérique: D'après les Six Osages actuellement à Paris, par M.P.V. Suivie de la relation du voyage de ces sauvages, et d'une notice historique sur chacune de ces indiens célèbres dans leur tribu par leurs exploits guerriers.* Paris, Chez Charles Béchet, Libraire, Quai des Augustins, No 57, et Chez Les Marchands Des Noveautés. A Rennes, Chez Duchesne, Libraire, Rue Royale, 1827.

Anonymous. *Notice Sur Les Six Indiens arrivés au Havre sur le Brick Américain le New-England, Le 27 Juillet 1827, dans laquelle se trouve la traduction littérale du discours adressé par leur Chef au Commandant de la Place, par une Personne qui est restée continuellement pres d'eux.* Paris, A la Librairie Française et Etrangère, Palais-Royal, Galeries de Bois, 1827.

Period Primary Sources

Anonymous. *Notice Sur Les Indiens arrivés à Paris le 13 Août 1827. Observations curieuses sur les moeurs et les coutumes de leur tribu guerrière.* Paris, Chez Martinet, Rue Du Coq-S-Honore, No. 15; Et Chez Delaunay, Au Palais-Royal, 1827. [Pamphlet of 14 pages.]

———. *Notice sur les Sauvages Arrivés des Bords du Missouri.* Paris, Imprimerie de C. Farcy, Rue de la Tabletterie, No. 9 [1827.] [Two pages.]

———. *Notice sur les Six Osages, arrivés à Paris le 13 Août 1827.* Prix: 40 Centimes. A Paris, Chez Tous Les Marchands De Nouveautés, 1827. [Pamphlet of 24 pages.]

———. *Bibliographie de la France, ou, Journal général de l'imprimerie et de la librairie et des cartes géographiques, gravures, lithographies, oeuvres de musique,* [for August and September 1827], Paris, 1811–1971.

———. "Indians of North America," unsigned review of John Dunn Hunter's *Manners and Customs of Several Indian Tribes Located West of the Mississippi. North American Review*, Volume XXII, New Series Volume XIII (1826), Boston, Mass.

P[aul]. v[on]. W[ürttemberg]. Untitled comment on Osages; no place or date of publication [1828].

Secondary Sources

Baird, W. David. *The Osage People.* Phoenix, Ariz.: Indian Tribal Series, 1972.

Barry, Louise. *The Beginning of the West: Annals of the Kansas Gateway to the American West 1540–1854.* Topeka: Kansas State Historical Society, 1972.

Berkhofer, Robert F., Jr. *The White Man's Indian: Images of the American Indian from Columbus to the Present*. New York: Knopf, 1978.

Biddle, Edward C. *Recommendatory Notices of the Indian History and Biography*. No place, 1837.

Billon, Frederic L. *Annals of St. Louis in Its Territorial Days from 1804 to 1821*. St. Louis, Mo.,1888.

Buckley, Jay H. *William Clark, Indian Diplomat*. Norman: University of Oklahoma Press, 2008.

Burns, Louis F. *A History of the Osage People*. Tuscaloosa: University of Alabama Press, 2004.

———. *Osage Indians: Customs and Myths*. Fallbrook, Calif.: Ciga Press, 1984.

Bushnell, David I., Jr. "Ethnographical Material from North America in Swiss Collections." *American Anthropologist*, new series, volume 10, number 1 (January–March 1908): 67.

Catlin, George. *Letters and Notes on the Manners, Customs, and Conditions of the North American Indians*. Two volumes. London, 1841.

Christensen, Lawrence O., William E. Foley, Gary R. Kremer, and Kenneth H. Winn, eds. *Dictionary of Missouri Biography*. Columbia: University of Missouri Press, 1999.

Clark, William. *Dear Brother: Letters of William Clark to Jonathan Clark*. James J. Holmberg, ed. New Haven, Conn.: Yale University Press, 2002.

———. "Letter to Thomas L. McKenney," June 7, 1830. In *United States Superintendency of Indian Affairs*, St. Louis Records, 1807–1855, volume 4. Topeka: Kansas State Historical Society.

———. "William Clark's Diary, May 1826–February 1831." Edited by Louise Barry. *Kansas State Historical Quarterly*, volume XVI, number 1 (February 1948).

Cortambert, Louis. "Journey to the Land of the Osages, 1835–1836." Translated by Mrs. Max W. Myer. *The Bulletin, Missouri Historical Society Collections*, volume XIX, number 3 (April 1963): 198–229.

Cosentino, Andrew J. *The Paintings of Charles Bird King (1785–1862)*. Washington, D.C.: Smithsonian Institution, 1977.

Dickason, Olive P. *The Myth of the Savage and the Beginnings of French Colonialism in the Americas*. Edmonton, Canada: University of Alberta Press, 1984.

Din, Gilbert C., and Abraham P. Nasatir. *The Imperial Osages: Spanish-Indian Diplomacy in the Mississippi Valley*. Norman: University of Oklahoma Press, 1983.

Drinnon, Richard. *White Savage: The Case of John Dunn Hunter*. New York: Schocken Books, 1972.

Dugatkin, Lee Alan. *Mr. Jefferson and the Giant Moose: Natural History in Early America*. Chicago: University of Chicago Press, 2009.

Ewers, John C. "'Chiefs from the Missouri and Mississippi' and Peale's Silhouettes of 1806." In *The Smithsonian Journal of History*, volume 1, number 1. Washington, D.C., spring 1966.

Fausz, J. Frederick. "Becoming 'A Nation of Quakers': The Removal of the Osage Indians from Missouri." *Gateway Heritage* (Summer 2000): 28–39.

Fletcher, Alice C. "The Osage in France." *American Anthropologist*, new series, volume 2, number 2 (April–June 1900): 395–99.

Foley, William E., and Charles David Rice. "Visiting the President: An Exercise in Jeffersonian Indian Diplomacy." *The American West* (November–December 1979): 4–15, 56.

Foreman, Carolyn Thomas. *Indians Abroad 1493–1938*. Norman: University of Oklahoma Press, 1943.

Foreman, Grant. "Our Indian Ambassadors to Europe." *Missouri Historical Society Collections*, volume V, number 2 (February 1928): 108–28.

Garraghan, Gilbert J. *Saint Ferdinand de Florissant: The Story of an Ancient Parish*. Chicago: Loyola University Press, 1923.

Hitchcock, Ethan Allen. *A Traveler in Indian Territory: The Journal of Ethan Allen Hitchcock, Late Major-General in the United States Army*. Grant Foreman, ed. Norman: University of Oklahoma Press, 1996 (reprint of 1930 Torch Press edition).

Hodge, Frederick Webb, ed. *Handbook of American Indians North of Mexico*, Part I. Bureau of American Ethnology, Bulletin 30 (1907), Washington, D.C., 927–29.

Hunter, John D. *Manners and Customs of Several Indian Tribes Located West of the Mississippi, Including Some Account of the Soil, Climate, and Vegetable Productions, and the Indian Materia Medica: To Which Is Prefixed the History of the Author's Life during a Residence of Several Years among Them*. Philadelphia, 1823.

———. *Memoirs of a Captivity among the Indians of North America, from Childhood to the Age of Nineteen, with Anecdotes Descriptive of Their Manners and Customs. To Which is Added Some Account of the Soil, Climate, and Vegetable Productions of the Territory Westward of the Mississippi*. Third Edition, with Additions. London, 1824.

———. *Memoirs of a Captivity among the Indians of North America*. Edited by Richard Drinnon. New York: Schocken Books, 1973.

Irving, Washington. *The Western Journals of Washington Irving*. Edited by John Francis McDermott. Norman: University of Oklahoma Press, 1944.

James, Edwin. "Account of an Expedition from Pittsburgh to the Rocky Mountains Performed in the Years 1819, 1820." In *Early Western Travels*, volume XIV. Edited by Reuben Gold Thwaites. Cleveland, 1905.

Janson, Charles William. *The Stranger in America, 1793–1806*. Edited by Carl S. Driver. New York: The Press of the Pioneers, 1935.

LaFlesche, Francis. *A Dictionary of the Osage Language*. Washington, D.C.: Government Printing Office, 1932.

———. "The Osage Tribe: Rite of the Chiefs, Sayings of the Ancient Men." *36th Annual Report of the Bureau of American Ethnology 1914–1915*. Washington, D.C., 1921.

———. *Traditions of the Osage: Stories Collected and Translated by Francis LaFlesche*. Edited by Garrick Bailey. Albuquerque: University of New Mexico Press, 2000.

Lewis, Meriwether. *The History of the Lewis and Clark Expedition*, Volume I. Edited by Elliott Coues. New York: Harper, 1893; reprinted 1964.

———. *The Journals of the Lewis & Clark Expedition*. Thirteen volumes. Edited by Gary E. Moulton. Lincoln: University of Nebraska Press, 1986–2001.

———. *Letters of the Lewis and Clark Expedition with Related Documents 1783–1854*. Two volumes, second edition. Edited by Donald Jackson. Urbana: University of Illinois Press, 1978.

———. *Original Journals of the Lewis and Clark Expedition*, Volume I. Edited by Reuben Gold Thwaites. 1904.

Malte-Brun, Conrad. *Précis de la Géographie universelle*. Eight volumes and atlas. Paris, 1810–1829.

Mathews, John Joseph. *The Osages: Children of the Middle Waters*. Norman: University of Oklahoma Press, 1961.

McKenney, Thomas L., and James Hall. *The Indian Tribes of North America, with Biographical Sketches and Anecdotes of the Principal Chiefs*. New edition, three volumes. Edinburgh, Scotland, 1933. [The first American edition, 1836, is titled *History of the Indian Tribes of North America*.]

McMillan, R. Bruce. "Perspectives on the Biogeography and Archaeology of

Bison in Illinois." In *Records of Early Bison in Illinois*. Scientific Papers 31. Springfield: Illinois State Museum, 2006.

McMillen, Margot Ford, and Heather Roberson. *Into the Spotlight: Four Missouri Women*. Columbia: University of Missouri Press, 2004.

McMillen, Margot Ford, ed., and Pippa Letsky, trans. "Les Indiens Osages: French Publicity for the Traveling Osage." *Missouri Historical Review*, volume XCVII, number 4 (June 2003). [A translated version of the third edition of *Six Indiens Rouges*.]

Miles, Ellen G. "Saint-Mémin's Portraits of American Indians, 1804–1807." *The American Art Journal*, volume XX, number 4 (1988): 3–33.

Morison, Samuel Eliot. *Admiral of the Ocean Sea: A Life of Christopher Columbus*. Two volumes. Boston: Atlantic Monthly Press, 1942.

———. *The European Discovery of America: The Northern Voyages, A.D. 500–1600*. New York, 1971.

Norall, Frank. *Bourgmont: Explorer of the Missouri 1698–1725*. Lincoln: University of Nebraska Press, 1988.

Nuttall, Thomas. *A Journal of Travels into the Arkansas Territory during the Year 1819*. Edited by Savoie Lottinville. Norman: University of Oklahoma Press, 1980.

Peake, Ora Brooks. *A History of the United States Indian Factory System 1795–1822*. Denver: Sage Books, 1954.

Peattie, Donald Culross. *A Natural History of Trees of Eastern and Central North America*. New York, 1948 and 1964.

Perrin, Nicolas. "Extraits et Analyses d'Ouvrages, *Memoirs of a Captivity*." In *Journal des Voyages*, volume 24 (October 1824): 64–99.

Pike, Zebulon Montgomery. *The Journals of Zebulon Montgomery Pike*. Volume I. Edited by Donald Jackson. Norman: University of Oklahoma Press, 1966.

Rollings, Willard H. *The Osage: An Ethnohistorical Study of Hegemony on the Prairie-Plains*. Columbia: University of Missouri Press, 1992.

Shoemaker, Floyd C., ed. "Missouriana: Mohongo's Story." *Missouri Historical Review*, volume 36, number 2 (January 1942): 21–214.

Stanley, John Mix. *Portraits of North American Indians, with Sketches of Scenery, Etc.* Washington, D.C., 1852 [appears in *Smithsonian Miscellaneous Collections*, Volume II, Washington, 1862].

Tixier, Victor. *Tixier's Travels on the Osage Prairies*. Edited by John Francis McDermott, translated by Albert J. Salvan. Norman: University of

Oklahoma Press, 1940.

Truettner, William H. *The Natural Man Observed: A Study of Catlin's Indian Gallery.* Washington, D.C.: Smithsonian Books, 1979.

————. *Painting Indians and Building Empires in North America 1710–1840.* Berkeley: University of California Press, 2010.

Viola, Herman J. *The Indian Legacy of Charles Bird King.* Washington, D.C.: Smithsonian Institution Press, 1976.

Wagner, Henry R., and Charles L. Camp. *The Plains & Rockies: A Critical Bibliography of Exploration, Adventure and Travel in the American West 1800–1865.* Fourth Edition Revised and Enlarged. San Francisco: John Howell, 1982.

Wilhelm, Paul, Duke of Württemberg. *Travels in North America 1822–1824.* Edited by Savoie Lottinville, translated by W. Robert Nitske. Norman: University of Oklahoma Press, 1973.

Wilson, Terry P. *Bibliography of the Osage.* Tuscaloosa: University of Alabama Press, 1985.

Wolferman, Kristie C. *The Osage in Missouri.* Columbia: University of Missouri Press, 1997.

Wood, W. Raymond. *Prologue to Lewis and Clark: The Mackay and Evans Expedition.* Norman: University of Oklahoma Press, 2003.

Nineteenth-Century News Accounts

The number of relevant nineteenth-century newspaper stories about the thirty-seven-month visit of the six Osages to Europe shall never be known in its entirety, but the several accounts listed here, many of them from Grant and Carolyn Foreman's two essays, we believe to be representative of the early legs of the tour.

Journal de Commerce, Paris, July 24, 1827.

L'Abeille, New Orleans, September 26, 1829.

L'Argus, New Orleans, May 1827.

La Quotidienne, Paris, August 1, 1827.

Le Courier, New Orleans, November 5, 1827.

Le Courier des Dames, Paris, August ?, 1827.

Le Courier des Pays-Bas, Brussels, December 26, 1827; February 20, 26, 1828; July 21, 1829.

Le Moniteur Universel, Paris, July 24, August 4, 11, 12, 15, 20, September 1, 1827; January 13, November 26, December 21, 1829.

Missouri Gazette, St. Louis, November 13, 1818.

Missouri Republican, St. Louis, October 18, November 1, 8, 15, 1827; January 17, 24, 1828.

New York Evening-Post, April 16, 1830.

Niles Weekly Register, Baltimore, September 5, 1829, page 19.

Index

Page numbers in italic type refer to illustrations.